COSTUME CLOSE-UP
Clothing Construction and Pattern
1750–1790

BY LINDA BAUMGARTEN & JOHN WATSON
with FLORINE CARR

The Colonial Williamsburg Foundation

Williamsburg, Virginia

In Association with
Quite Specific Media Group Ltd.
New York and Hollywood

©1999 by The Colonial Williamsburg Foundation

Second printing, 2000

Published by The Colonial Williamsburg Foundation, Williamsburg, Virginia, in association with
Quite Specific Media Group Ltd., Hollywood, California

Costume & Fashion Press
an imprint of
Quite Specific Media Group Ltd.
7373 Pyramid Place
Hollywood, California 90046

Business Office
(212) 725-5377 phone; (212) 725-8506 fax
email: info@quitespecificmedia.com

Other Quite Specific Media Group Ltd. imprints:
Drama Publishers
By Design Press
EntertainmentPro
Jade Rabbit

On-line catalog:
http://www.quitespecificmedia.com

Library of Congress Cataloging-in-Publication Data

Baumgarten, Linda.
    Costume close-up : clothing construction and pattern, 1750–1790 /
by Linda Baumgarten and John Watson, with Florine Carr.
    p.   cm.
    ISBN 0-87935-188-8 (CW). — ISBN 0-89676-226-2 (QSM)
    1. Costume design—History—18th century. 2. Costume—History—18th century. 3. Colonial
Williamsburg Foundation Catalogs. I. Watson, John, 1952–   . II. Carr, Florine. III. Title.
TT507.B38, 1999
646.4'78—dc21   99-33258
                                                                                                            CIP

Book Design: John R. Watson
Color Insert Design: Helen Mageras
Photography: Hans Lorenz and Craig McDougal

Front Cover: Cloak no. 21
Back Cover: Gown no. 2

Printed in Hong Kong

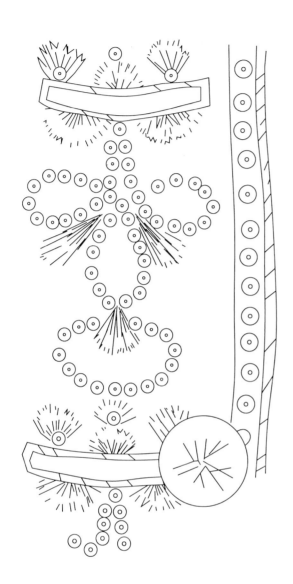

❦ CONTENTS

❧ Side Topics

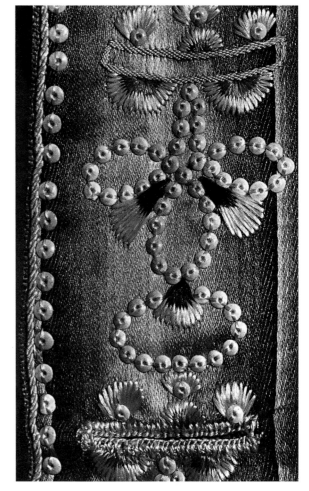

Detail, waistcoat no. 20.

🐝 INTRODUCTION

The Language of Clothing

Antique objects in a museum collection are very much like rare books in a library. Although artifacts do not speak with words, they are no less compelling in their ability to talk to us. When we can translate their language, they tell wonderful stories and reveal volumes about the past. This book looks closely at antique clothing to explore what it tells us about cut, fit, and construction. The study focuses on twenty-five pieces of clothing or ensembles from the second half of the eighteenth century now in the permanent collections of the Colonial Williamsburg Foundation in Williamsburg, Virginia.

This book is less about how to sew modern copies than about how to look at antique clothing to uncover its lessons. Curators, conservators, costumers, and reenactors today seek to understand the intricacies of eighteenth-century clothing construction and fit, not just its superficial appearance. Although the talented seamstress or tailor with advanced skills will be able to construct reproductions using the information in this book, exact copies of eighteenth-century clothing will seldom fit or look the same on the modern person.

Body shape and posture have changed in the past two hundred years because of a combination of body-molding clothing, lessons in posture and deportment, and habits of exercise. Stays—worn by most women from childhood—had the effect of molding the female torso into an inverted cone without individual cups for the bosom. Stays were laced on the body over a linen shift. They pushed the fullness of the breasts up and urged the shoulders back and down, creating very erect posture. Those women who were considered beautiful had slim arms and sloping shoulders. Although a small waist was desirable, the ideal silhouette was not the constricted hourglass of the mid-nineteenth century. (Notice the waist sizes of the gowns shown in this book.) The eighteenth-century ideal was a tapering line from midbust to waist. Fitted gowns were built over the smooth line of the stays without the darts typical of nineteenth-century clothing.

The fashionable man's body of 1750 to 1790 also had sloping shoulders, a narrow back, and slim, nonmuscular upper arms. Square shoulders were not considered desirable, and thick shoulder pads were not used in men's suits. Rather, padding enhanced (or created) a prominent chest. The cut of the suit also emphasized the chest and stomach by placing shoulder and underarm seams toward the back, strengthening the illusion.

Posture and body shape have changed over time. At the left is the erect posture, cone-shaped torso, and triangular silhouette of the 1750s. The center illustration shows the small waists and rounded shoulders of the 1840s. On the right is the boyish figure of the 1920s.

Clothing gives us a picture of the past—not just a still photograph but a moving picture. Decorative arts are subject to the vicissitudes of time and ownership, but clothing is one of the most likely to experience significant change over time. An old-fashioned chair can be relegated to an upstairs bedchamber, where it remains quietly useful without alteration. An item of clothing, on the other hand, cannot serve its original purpose (as clothing) unless it is still in fashion and fits the new owner. Even if it has been put away for preservation, it might be brought out of retirement and taken in or let out for wear at a family wedding, a centenary ball, or a theatrical event. Every act of changing a seam, lengthening a hem, removing trim, treating a stain, or patching a hole leaves its tracks on a garment, tells about the succession of people who used it, and becomes part of its future.

In analyzing an antique garment, we not only stand back to assess and admire its style and artistic accomplishment but we also look with a close lens at old stitch marks, folds, loose threads from re-moved trimmings, and patterns of fading and wear. Every fold and stitch hole is part of a puzzle. So much information resides in an artifact that any one item of clothing in this volume could be the subject of its own book; we are able to cover only the highlights. Those of us given the privilege of caring for antique costumes need to be especially aware of our impact on such collections and sensitive to the potential for obscuring and even obliterating historical information, some of which we may not yet recognize as important. It goes without saying that the authors did not take any garments apart to develop the patterns, and there are probably some resulting inaccuracies in measurements and incomplete construction notes. Our tools were both ancient and modern—pencils, tape measures, graph paper, tracing paper, microscopes, and computers.

Old garments—*costumes,* as they are often called—have a particular ability to engage us. After all, they were worn by living human beings whose bodies left their impressions in the very fabric of the pieces. These were people who had to make choices about how to spend their money, how they wanted (or needed) to be seen, what they considered beautiful, and what they thought was appropriate for their age and station in life. Many had to cope with gaining or losing weight, getting pregnant, working hard, and making do with limited re-sources. They watched the fashions and the fashion-able for clues about whether they were keeping up. And almost everyone had their clothing remodeled or remade in response to life's changing conditions.

Alterations

The story of a piece of eighteenth-century clothing didn't usually end when it was packed away because it looked a little shabby or was hopelessly out of fashion. The expense of these hand-woven textiles

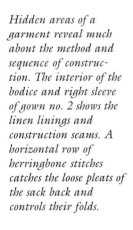

Hidden areas of a garment reveal much about the method and sequence of construc-tion. The interior of the bodice and right sleeve of gown no. 2 shows the linen linings and construction seams. A horizontal row of herringbone stitches catches the loose pleats of the sack back and controls their folds.

dictated that useful cloth was salvaged whenever possible by mending and patching, retrimming the garment to make it look different, taking in or letting out seams, cutting it down so it could be worn by a child, or taking it apart entirely to start over. Clothing was left in wills to be worn by successive generations. Very few eighteenth-century garments have survived without some alterations in their history. Indeed, some were made with future alteration in mind. (Notice especially the skirts in the three gowns in this volume.) In today's era of plentiful textiles, we give little thought to future remodeling, considering it cheaper to buy new than to go to the trouble of altering our clothing—unless it is a very favorite old piece or a family heirloom such as a wedding dress.

Construction Methods

Besides the story of change over time, eighteenth-century clothing also reveals much about the technology of the period. Clothing construction methods were very different two hundred years ago. There were no sewing machines, safety pins, or zippers. The approach to fitting and sewing a piece of clothing differed in three ways from that used in home and factory sewing today. First, all sewing was done by hand. Second, textiles were very expensive and less plentiful, requiring frugal use of materials. Finally, much clothing was fitted to the wearer's body during construction rather than sewn together from standardized pattern pieces.

Today, we begin with a full-size pattern of the proper size, lay the pattern pieces on our cloth, and cut them out. We follow different cutting layouts for different widths of fabric and make sure that all of the pieces have the grain running in the right direction, usually with the warp up and down on the body. We might buy an extra yard of material to ensure that the nap goes in the right direction and that all of the pattern pieces fit properly on the goods without piecing.

Eighteenth-century clothing construction followed different rules. The cost of fabric usually exceeded that of labor in a garment, so more time and effort were expended to save textiles, even if it meant arduously splicing a piece together from smaller scraps. The nap direction of the fabric mattered less than economizing on the yardage used. Several eighteenth-century velvet and plush breeches in the Williamsburg collection have different nap direction on the front and the back of the leg, quite visible at the side seams where the two textiles join.

Today, most seams are sewn by machine with the right sides together, leaving seam allowances of about ⅝" (16 mm). The seams are pressed, graded, notched, or clipped so that they lie flat when they are turned, then they are pressed again. Facings

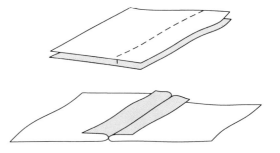

Modern seams usually are stitched by machine with right sides together, leaving wide seam allowances that are pressed open.

neatly finish most outside edges, and generous hems ensure that the onlooker doesn't see the back, or "wrong," side of the textile. In the eighteenth century, almost all seam allowances and hems were small, ranging from ⅛" (3 mm) to about ⅜" (10 mm). Instead of leaving large seam allowances to accommodate raveling in the wash, garments intended to be laundered had their narrow seams laboriously finished to enclose all raw edges.

Today, we use strips of fabric cut on the bias to bind edges. In the eighteenth century, bindings were cut on the straight of the goods. Certainly the extreme waste of material that results from cutting bias binding would have been unacceptable in the 1700s. In fact, it may not have occurred to eighteenth-century seamstresses and tailors to try it. It is difficult to manipulate straight-grain binding around curves with a machine. When working by hand, one can make adjustments and ease the textiles together.

Today, linings are usually cut to their own individual pattern pieces, sewn separately, and inserted into the garment near the end of construction. In the eighteenth century, linings were usually cut to the same shape as the main pattern pieces. The fashion fabric and lining were often treated as one during the initial construction. This practice was especially true for men's clothing. Seldom were linings set in as a separate step at the end. In fact, for women's gowns, the bodice lining often came first, forming the foundation on which the entire bodice was draped and stitched.

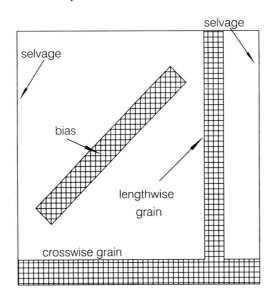

Straight-grain binding versus bias binding. The lengthwise grain runs parallel to the selvages in a textile. This is the warp direction. The crosswise grain is the weft. The true bias is cut on a 45° angle to the warp and weft and is stretchy.

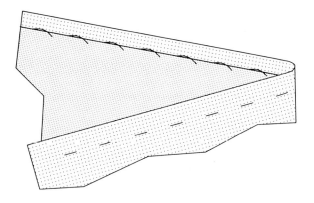

Separate facings were seldom used two hundred years ago. Rather, linings extended out to the edges of the garment, where they were turned under and stitched to the fashion fabric. This process was often done with a stitch that resembles slanted hemming stitch on the lining side but forms running topstitching on the fashion fabric side. This stitching method sews the parts together and topstitches in one operation. It is the stitch illustrated in the eighteenth-century French *Encyclopédie* by Denis Diderot and called *le point à rabattre sous la main*, sometimes translated as the underhand hem stitch. (See sketch above.)

The man's silk suit coat in number 17 (below) is a good case in point. The seams suggest that the order of assembly for the main body parts differed from modern construction. First, the coat front and back were cut and pieced out to the proper width, since the silk textile measured only about 21" (53.3 cm) wide—typical for patterned silk during this period. The interfacings, paddings, pockets,

buttons, and buttonholes were worked into each coat front, apparently before the side seams were sewn. At this point, each front and back piece must have received its silk lining, leaving the vertical seams at the underarms and center back free, or perhaps basted. The slashes for the back and side pleats were cut through both the lining and front layers. After sewing the vertical seams (joining front to back and back to back), the skirts were pleated, manipulating the lining and fashion fabric together for the pleating process. The pleats were tacked in place on the inside of the coat, and the outside was reinforced and finished off neatly with a decorative button at the top of the pleats. The linen and cotton lining material for the upper back was laid over the silk linings, turned under, and stitched in place to the silk linings. Clearly, this is a different approach from today's method of sewing the outer coat and the lining as two separate garments.

The technique of draping is fundamental to the construction and fit of eighteenth-century women's gowns. On each of the three gowns included in this book, the bodice back was cut in one piece with the skirt and pleated. Whether left as loose pleats to form a sack back or stitched down to the lining, the fitting was done directly on the wearer's body.

Evidence in the seams and linings of the lavender polonaise gown (no. 3) shows how the sleeves were set in to fit the individual wearer. One side of the sleeve's underarm seam was turned under and lapped over the area to be joined, then sewn with backstitches through all layers close to the edge. (See the upper sketch in the illustration below.) This is an obvious way to do the seam if one is working directly on the body, pinning or sewing from the outside. Further, the lined and seamed sleeves were initially set into the lined bodice under the arms only, leaving the caps free to be smoothed and tucked to fit over the woman's shoulders. The tucks were then held down by the separate shoulder straps laid over the top of the arms. The shoulder

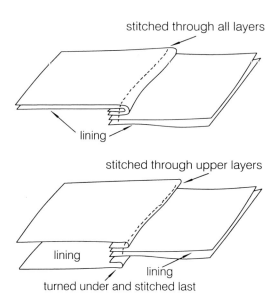

stitched through all layers

lining

stitched through upper layers

lining

lining

turned under and stitched last

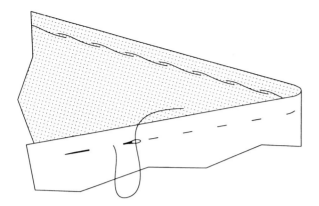

Two stitches used to construct clothing in the eighteenth century. To the left is the back-stitch; to the right, the running stitch.

straps were stitched from the outside, joining the bodice front and back pieces as well as fastening the tucked sleeves into place. It is almost impossible to set in this style of sleeve without doing so in two separate steps and on a three-dimensional form or human body.

An alternative sometimes seen in bodice seams was to lap and sew the top three layers, leaving the bottom lining free to be turned under and neatly finished off later, thus hiding all raw edges. (See the illustration on the lower right of p. 8.) This technique contrasts with modern sewing-machine construction, in which right sides are put together and seamed, then turned right side out.

Seams

Despite their visual elaboration, eighteenth-century clothes were constructed with a limited repertoire of seam stitches. The choice of stitch was logical and practical, depending on whether the seam would receive stress, whether the garment would be laundered, and whether it might be taken apart for later alterations. Shirts and shifts were sewn with fine backstitches and then felled to enclose all raw edges. Linen selvages were joined by butting and whipstitching them closely. This process not only saved expensive fabric but resulted in sturdy garments that could withstand washing.

Men's fitted coats, waistcoats, and breeches were sewn with sturdy backstitches that withstood the strain of movement. Unless extra strength was needed, the backstitches were spaced so that the individual stitches did not touch, thus speeding the sewing work.

Because gowns were likely to be taken apart for alteration or redying, their skirt seams typically were sewn with long running stitches secured with an occasional backstitch. The gowns in this study have seams with 5 to 9 running stitches per inch (2.5 cm). Full skirts did not receive much stress, and the long running stitches were easy to rip out when a gown was remodeled. The bodice and sleeve seams of gowns often were lapped and sewn from the top with spaced backstitches, as described on page 8. This technique gave greater strength and was easier to construct from the body out. Closely worked backstitches were used to set sleeves into the lower half of the armscye. This stitch provided greater durability.

Acknowledgments

The research and designing of this book were supported by a generous grant from Mrs. Pleasant Rowland of Pleasant Company. All photographs are by Hans Lorenz. The authors also thank their friends and colleagues for encouragement and assistance. Special recognition goes to Colleen Callahan, Sandy Carr, Suzanne Coffman, Kathleen Epstein, Loreen Finklestein, Nancy Glass, Carol Harrison, Richard Hill, Ronald Hurst, Kimberly Smith Ivey, Claudia Brush Kidwell, Carol Kocian, Santina Levy, Helen Mageras, Mark Hutter, Craig McDougal, Scott Nolley, Carolyn Randall, Brenda Rosseau, Doris Warren, and Janea Whitacre. Colonial Williamsburg's collections and conservation activities are supported in part by the DeWitt Wallace Fund for Colonial Williamsburg. 🎗

❦ CONVENTIONS

The lines and symbols on the pattern pages are standardized to follow the chart below. Main pattern pieces are shown with bold outlines. Seam allowances are not included in the pattern pieces. Linings are not always shown separately, especially where they are cut to the same pattern as the main piece. The grain line symbol represents the lengthwise grain, or *warp*, of the textile where it was possible to determine it. The grain lines of a pattern piece are usually aligned perpendicular or parallel to the paper's edge.

We have chosen to show the patterns to one of four scales, selected to accommodate the size of the garments and their clarity on the page. In this era of enlarging copying machines and computer scanners, it seemed less important to show the patterns on standard graph paper.

Drawings and pattern outlines are of the actual antique garments and reflect the piecing, alterations, stitching errors, stretching, and shrinking that have occurred over the years. The pieces have not been idealized or sized to fit the modern body.

The terms *proper left* or *proper right* are used in the text and drawings to refer to the wearer's left or right, as opposed to those of the viewer.

The number listed in the upper left corner of the pattern page is the museum accession number—the permanent number by which we link an object and its records. The number is also visible in some of the photographs on an applied tag. Any inquiry about an artifact should include this number. The first four numbers are the year the museum acquired the object, and the numbers after the dash reflect the order in which it was acquired. ❦

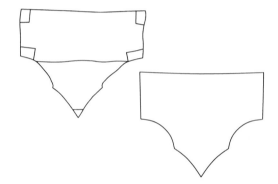

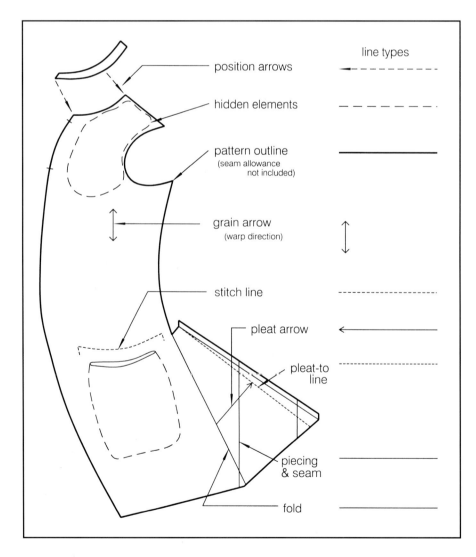

line types

position arrows — – – – – –

hidden elements — – – – – –

pattern outline
(seam allowance not included) ▬▬▬▬

grain arrow
(warp direction) ↕

stitch line - - - - - - - -

pleat arrow ←————

pleat-to line - - - - - - - -

piecing & seam ————

fold ————

1

GOWN AND STOMACHER

England, ca. 1756, remodeled from earlier gown

Cream silk satin; linen lining; linen and silk sewing threads

Gown: Length, 56" (142.2 cm); back shoulder width, 10" (25.4 cm); satin selvage width, 21¼" (54 cm)
   Skirt front length, 36" (91.4 cm); skirt hem circumference, 140¼" (356.2 cm)
   Chest without stomacher, 29–30" (73.7–76.2 cm); chest with stomacher, approximately 41" (104.1 cm)
   Waist without stomacher, 25–26" (63.5–66 cm); waist with stomacher, approximately 31" (78.7 cm)
Stomacher: 13¼" high × 12" wide (33.7 × 30.5 cm)

Accession number: 1985-117, 1-2

Hinkley in 1756. Although the gown is English, related styles were certainly worn in America. In a 1758 painting by John Singleton Copley, a young Massachusetts girl named Elizabeth Royall wears a white satin gown that is pinked and punched like the sleeve ruffles and applied trim in this example.

Materials

The gown is made of heavy, cream-color silk satin. The selvages are striped with green silk and metallic threads. The bodice and sleeves are lined with white plain-woven linen, 64 by 64 threads per inch (2.5 cm). The gown is sewn with linen, and the trim is applied with silk. The stomacher is made of thin plain-woven silk and lined with linen 96 by 80 threads per inch (2.5 cm); it is trimmed with pinked self-fabric.

Change over Time

Pick marks, thread remnants, and piecing on the gown indicate that it was remade from an older garment that had generous sleeves and elaborate

Left: Silk satin gown and stomacher, shown with quilted petticoat no. 5.

Many gowns of the mid- to late eighteenth century shared a similar style, gaining their distinction from the textiles and applied trimmings rather than changes in basic cut. This gown represents one popular style option. It has a low neckline, separate triangular stomacher at the open front of a cone-shaped bodice; elbow-length, flounced sleeves; and a full skirt open in front to reveal the petticoat underneath. The back is pleated and sewn down to the lining, close to the body, a style that contrasts with the looser *sack back* featured in number 2.

According to oral tradition, the gown was the wedding dress of Ursula Westof, a Leicester, England, woman who married John Robinson of

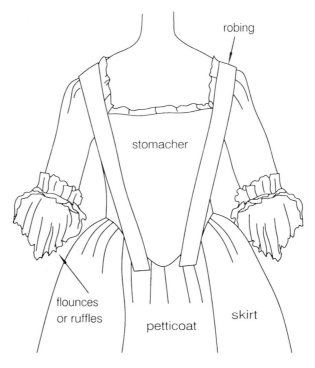

Parts of an eighteenth-century gown. The stomacher and petticoat are separate pieces.

robing

stomacher

flounces or ruffles

petticoat

skirt

trimmings. The very wide seam allowances of the sleeves still retain the folded edges of the original seam allowances. The material itself further supports the internal evidence of remodeling. Rich silk satin was favored for women's gowns in the 1740s, about ten or fifteen years before this gown was remade into a newer style. There are scattered stains. Many seams and much of the trimming have been restitched with modern thread. Tape is stitched to the back inside waist. Intended to be brought around to the front and tied to hold the back waist snugly to the body, this tape is of more recent origin, judging from its fresh color and condition. No petticoat survives with the gown.

Gown Construction

Stitching: The gown is constructed with running stitches, backstitches, slip stitches, and slanted stitches using linen thread. The skirt is sewn with linen running stitches, 5 per inch (2.5 cm). Occasionally a backstitch was worked to give extra strength at the seams. The underarm portions of the sleeves are set into the bodice with backstitches. The trimmings are sewn on with silk.

Bodice Back: Like most other women's gowns of the eighteenth century, this one was fitted while draped on the body. The bodice back was cut in one piece with the center back skirt and pleated directly on

the figure. The pleats are sewn down to a linen lining with running stitches that end just below the waist. The fullness is released into the skirt by means of pleats at the lower waist. The excess textile at the center back seam was trimmed away to give a seam allowance of ³⁄₈" to ½" (1 to 1.3 cm). The back neckline was finished by turning the satin and the linen lining to the inside toward each other and stitching with running stitches.

Skirt: The full, pleated skirt consists of seven panels of silk, seamed at the selvages and left unlined. Some of the skirt panels were pieced together from the remodeling process. Excess skirt length not needed because of the dip in the bodice waist was folded down and pleated through the fold, not cut off. Leaving the excess length made future alterations easier. The skirt pleats vary from 1½" to 2" (3.8 to 5 cm) deep, with about 1" (2.5 cm) showing on the outside. The waist seam has visible slanted stitches on the outside. The stitching indicates that the skirt was attached from the right side, most likely pleated to fit while on the body. The satin of the bodice waist seam allowance was turned under and apparently stitched to the skirt as each pleat was formed. On the inside, the raw upper edges of the skirt pleats were enclosed in the linen bodice lining, turned under, and stitched. The pleats are directed toward the pocket slits at the

Interior of gown bodice showing linen lining and piecing of skirt. The ribbon sewn to the back waistline was added later.

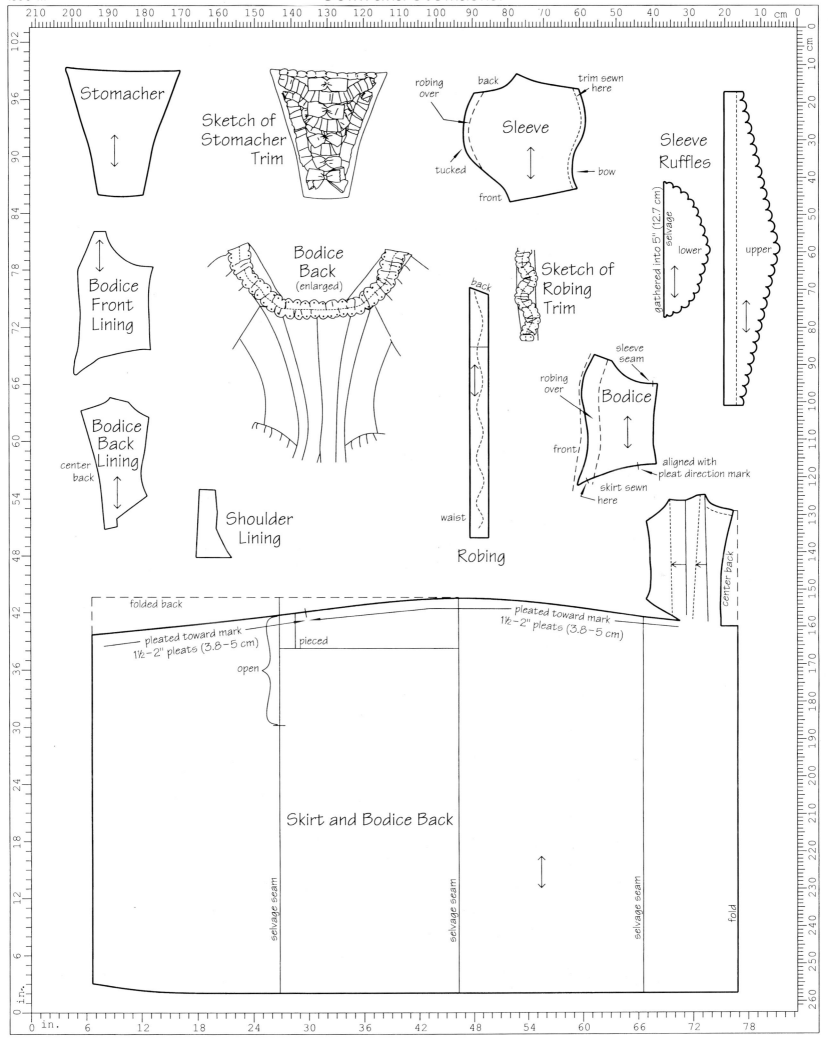

Stomacher

Sketch of
Stomacher
Trim

Sleeve

robing
over

back

trim sewn
here

tucked

front

bow

Sleeve
Ruffles

gathered into 5" (12.7 cm)

selvage

lower

upper

Bodice
Front
Lining

Bodice
Back
(enlarged)

Sketch of
Robing
Trim

back

Bodice

robing
over

sleeve
seam

front

Bodice
Back
Lining

center
back

Shoulder
Lining

Robing

waist

aligned with
pleat direction mark

skirt sewn
here

center back

Skirt and Bodice Back

folded back

pleated toward mark
1½–2" pleats (3.8–5 cm)

pieced

open

pleated toward mark
1½–2" pleats (3.8–5 cm)

selvage seam

selvage seam

selvage seam

fold

sides. The skirt front is open to reveal a petticoat worn underneath. The front edges were hemmed by turning under the selvages and stitching them with running stitches. The pocket slits are 11½" (29.2 cm) long, hemmed by turning the selvages under and sewing them with running stitches. The bottom hem is faced on the back side with pieces from two different ribbons and scraps of satin. These hem facings measure about 1" (2.5 cm) wide and are stitched at the bottom and the top with running stitches.

Bodice Front: As is usual for the period, the bodice has no darts. The smooth cone produced by the stays underneath meant that bust darts were not necessary. The bodice front has an overlay of decorative robings, tacked in place and extending over the shoulders to the back. The robings are made from sewn tubes of satin, flattened with the seam concealed on the bottom side. Hidden under the robings at the front, the raw edges of the satin bodice are turned under and stitched with running stitches to the linen lining, which extends slightly beyond the satin. The linen gives a sturdy extension for pinning the stomacher in place, yet the pins are hidden by the robings. The front bodice pieces are lapped over the back bodice at the sides and the seams sewn from the top with backstitches through both of the fashion fabrics and one lining. The remaining lining piece was turned under and sewn last. (See illustration, p. 8.)

Punched and pinked trimming on bodice front robing.

How was pinking done?

Pinking was done with a pinking iron, a metal tool with sharp edges of the desired shape for the finished design. The textile was folded and positioned under the cutting edge of the pinking iron. The pinking tool was struck with a mallet, cutting down through the layers of fabric. Because period silks were very finely woven, the pinked edges did not ravel significantly. This pinking iron probably dates to the eighteenth century.

Bodice Trim: The robings and back neckline are trimmed with satin ruching. The ruching consists of a strip of the dress fabric from 1½" to 1⅞" (3.8 to 4.8 cm) wide, pinked with scallops at the edges and punched with eyelets. Because of the pinking, there is no hem or other finish on the trimming. The pinked trimming is gathered down the center and tacked to the robings in a serpentine pattern with running stitches. The pinked trimming continues around the back of the neck, beyond the robing, and over the back neck binding.

Sleeves: The elbow-length sleeves are fully lined with linen. The satin is cut on the cross of the fabric, with warps running around the arm instead of lengthwise. The sleeve seams are lapped and stitched from the outside with widely spaced backstitches through all layers of the satin and the linen lining. (See illustration, p. 8.) The seam allowances range from 1½" to 2" (3.8 to 5 cm). The excess fabric from the older, fuller sleeves remains in place inside the sleeve. One can still see the folds and stitch holes from the original sleeve seams before the gown was remodeled. The armscye

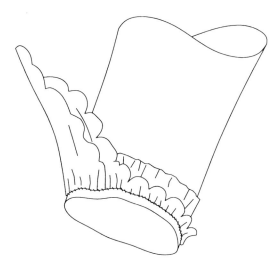

seams are sewn with backstitches, leaving the cap free. The cap was pleated to the correct shape over the wearer's shoulder while the gown was draped on her body. The robing piece was laid in place over the pleated sleeve cap and stitched down to cover the raw edges. The shoulder lining pieces are roughly stitched in place on the gown interior with running and slip stitches. The lined sleeves were finished at the ends by turning the raw edges of satin and linen to the inside toward each other and sewing with running stitch.

Sleeve Trim: Each sleeve has two ruffles sewn to the sleeve opening. The ruffles were gathered together and applied to the end of the sleeve after it was seamed and lined. This double ruffle is tacked onto the end of the sleeve from the underside. That is, the gathered ruffles were folded at the gathering stitches, positioned at the sleeve opening, flipped up, and whipstitched in place. The gathered straight edge on the upper ruffle is running stitched around

the sleeve itself, forming a decorative band above the scalloped flounces that fall gracefully over the elbows. A silk bow ornaments the inside of each sleeve at the crook of the arm. The bow is made from 24" (61 cm) of 1⅜" (3.5 cm) wide pinked satin and tied together with a narrower piece of ribbed silk ribbon. The bows are tacked to the sleeves inside the elbows.

Stomacher Construction

The front of the gown is filled with a triangular stomacher elaborately trimmed to match the gown. The thin silk is backed with fine linen brought up to the edges, turned under, and slip-stitched. The stomacher is not interlined or stiffened. The trimmings are made of the satin gown fabric, cut with the grain in three different widths, pinked, gathered, and stitched in place through the silk ground and linen backing. The satin "ribbons" are cut 1⅜" wide, ⅝" wide, and ¾" wide (3.5, 1.6, and 1.9 cm). Holes in the edges of the stomacher show that it was pinned in place to the gown. 🪡

Interior of shoulder and sleeve armscye showing the linen lining pieces.

Upper left: *The ruffle was sewn from the underside and allowed to fall over the stitching.*

Lower left: *Sleeve, lined with linen and trimmed with scalloped, pinked ruffles and bow.*

2

GOWN, STOMACHER, AND PETTICOAT

England, 1770–1780

Multicolor brocaded silk; linen and silk linings; linen tape; silk fringe trim; linen and silk sewing threads

Gown: Length, 64" (162.6 cm); back shoulder width, 10¼" (26 cm); silk selvage width, 19⅞" (50.5 cm)
   Skirt hem circumference, 98½" (250.2 cm)
    Chest without stomacher, 28¾" (73 cm); chest with stomacher, approximately 37" (94 cm)
    Waist without stomacher, 21" (53.3 cm); waist with stomacher, approximately 25" (63.5 cm)
Petticoat: Skirt front length, 36" (91.4 cm); hem circumference, 108½" (275.6 cm); waist, 23" (58.4 cm)
Stomacher: 14¾" high × 11" wide (37.5 × 27.9 cm)

Accession number: G1991-472 a-c, Gift of Cora Ginsburg

Gown overall with skirt buttoned up in polonaise fashion.

This gown illustrates the best qualities of its period—lively and colorful brocaded silk piled with crisp ruffles, ruching, and fringe. The effect is one of great elaboration and richness. The gown was worn with a stomacher, creating a low, squared neckline. The skirt is open to show the matching petticoat. Gowns with pleats falling from the back shoulders were called *sacks* in England and America. This graceful style was fashionable during much of the eighteenth century and was replaced only gradually by fitted styles during the last quarter of the

century, and by classical styles later. This example combines the sack back with the polonaise design, in which the skirt is drawn up in a drapery effect. The drapery theme continues into the petticoat. The petticoat's ruffle can be drawn up with buttons and loops, echoing those of the gown skirt. The name "Mary Nisbet" is roughly embroidered in red inside the bodice lining. The embroidered name dates from the nineteenth century and probably represents a later owner who inherited the gown.

Materials

The gown and matching petticoat are made of heavy ribbed silk woven with a striped subpattern using both warp and weft floats and brocaded with red, pink, and green flowers. The trimmings consist of pleated and gathered strips of the same fabric edged with silk looped fringe tape. All of the trimmings for the gown and petticoat are sewn with silk; the remaining seams are sewn with natural-color linen thread. Two different qualities of plain-woven linen are used for the gown lining. Five hooks made of flattened brass wire are stitched to the right front bodice opening; no corresponding eyelets survive. These hooks may date from the nineteenth century. The back of the petticoat is made of ribbed silk lined with linen. It has a linen tape waistband. The stomacher is cream silk brocaded with multicolor flowers, berries, and leaves on a floral subpattern and overlaid with fabric puffs and silk fringe. Neither the trim nor the brocaded silk match the gown.

Change over Time

The gown appears virtually unaltered. The colors are fresh and unfaded. The silk skirt facing, however, is very fragile, having been subject to abrasion against the petticoat or floor over the years. The back of the petticoat, not seen while worn, is pieced out with plain silk, and the lining may be a slightly later addition. Unlike the gown, the petticoat has been altered slightly at the waist, made smaller by

Gown and Stomacher

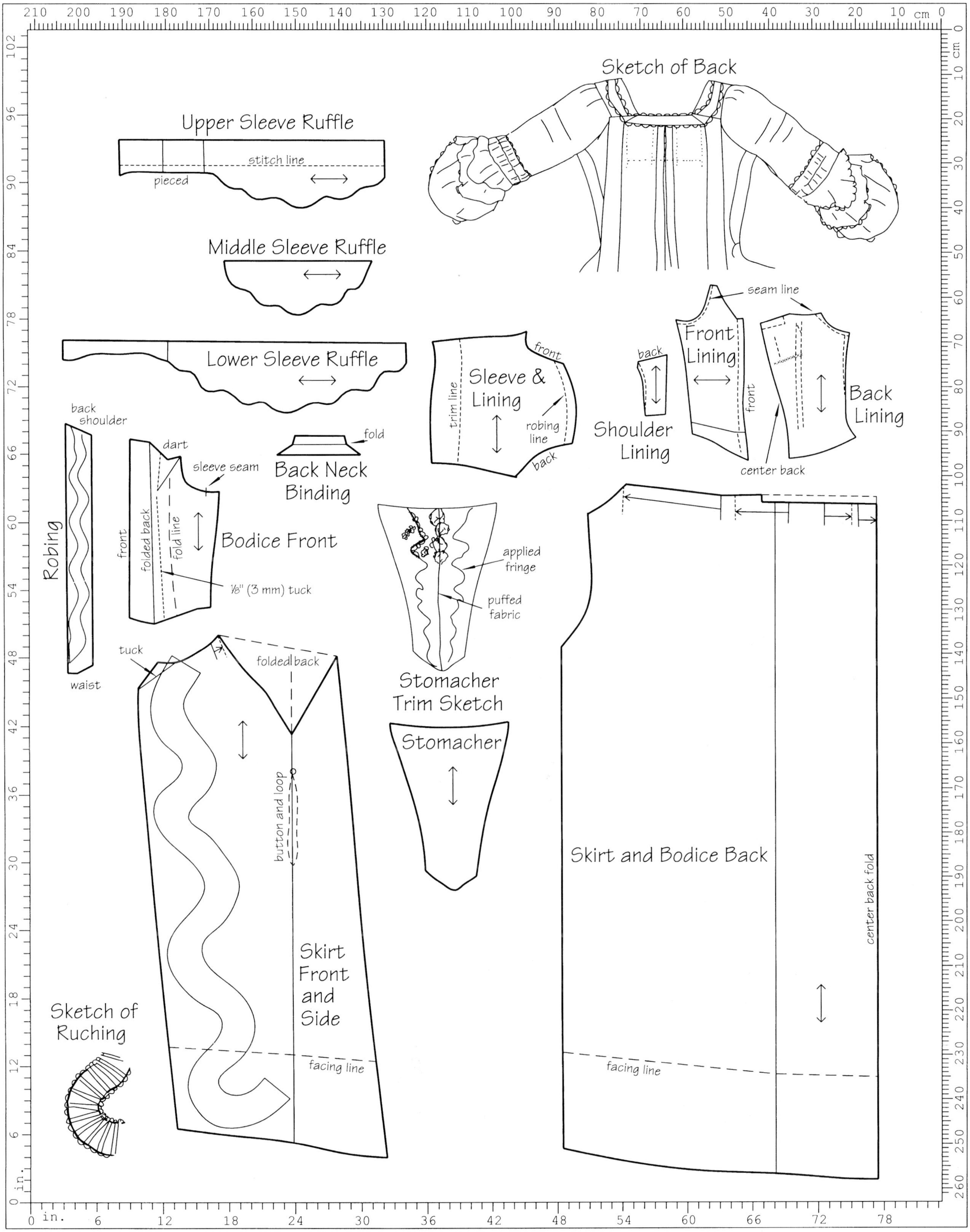

Upper Sleeve Ruffle

stitch line

pieced

Sketch of Back

Middle Sleeve Ruffle

Lower Sleeve Ruffle

fold

Back Neck Binding

seam line

back

Front Lining

front

Back Lining

Shoulder Lining

center back

trim line

Sleeve & Lining

front

robing line

back

back shoulder

dart

sleeve seam

front

folded back

fold line

Bodice Front

⅛" (3 mm) tuck

Robing

waist

applied fringe

puffed fabric

Stomacher Trim Sketch

Stomacher

tuck

folded back

button and loop

Skirt Front and Side

Sketch of Ruching

facing line

Skirt and Bodice Back

center back fold

facing line

adding extra pleats in the skirt. The twill tape waistband is a replacement. The stomacher does not match the rest of the ensemble and is either from another gown or is a later stomacher made from antique materials.

Gown Construction

Stitching: The gown is constructed with running stitches, backstitches, whipstitches, and slanted hemming stitches. The skirt seams are sewn with 5 to 6 running stitches per inch (2.5 cm). There are a few backstitches to help strengthen the seams. The side bodice and sleeve seams are backstitched from the outside. (See sketches, p. 8.)

Bodice Back: Like the other gowns discussed here, this one was draped and fitted on the body, and its pattern details and construction reflect that process. The bodice lining fits closely to the body with a center back seam that is butted and whipstitched.

The bodice back was cut in one piece with the back skirt and pleated directly on the body. The back pleats are very deep, sewn in position through to the lining about 4" (10.2 cm) down from the neckline using long running stitches and herringbone stitches. (See photograph, p. 6.) The close fit of the bodice lining holds the outer gown in position, tight to the chest in front but allowing the pleats to fall at the back. Although some sack-back gowns have adjustable linings that lace up the center back under the pleats, this example cannot be adjusted.

Neckline Finishing: The center back neck is bound with a shaped piece of brocaded silk that is folded over the raw edges of the lining and pleats. The edges of the binding are turned under and stitched with slanted hemming stitches. The neck binding does not extend to the extreme edges of the pleats; the outer pleats have their raw edges turned under and stitched to the robings.

Gown interior showing fitted linen lining and the back side of the brocaded textile. For a closer view, see p. 6.

Bodice Front: The cone-shaped bodice has a shaping dart at the shoulder that comes in toward the bust from the sleeve. The dart is hidden under the flap created by folding the bodice front edge back with the right sides together. The robing is a separate piece made from a single layer of brocaded silk. Its ½" (1.3 cm) seam allowances are folded to the back, where they are covered by thin silk lining. The lined robing strip is stitched to the edges of the bodice front fold, and the two are stitched down to the bodice. The robings extend up over the shoulders. The bodice is lined with two different qualities of plain-woven linen. The shoulder lining partially covers the silk; it was inserted and roughly stitched after the sleeve was set in.

Bodice Trim: The robing is trimmed with looped silk fringe and stitched in a parallel serpentine pattern to echo the lines on the skirt trim.

Sleeves: The sleeves are lined with linen matching that of the bodice. The silk is cut on the cross grain of the fabric, with warps running around the arm instead of lengthwise. The sleeve seams are lapped and topstitched with widely spaced backstitches through all layers, leaving seam allowances of ¾" to 1" (1.9 to 2.5 cm). The technique is illustrated on page 8. The sleeves are sewn into the armscye under the arm with backstitches for extra strength. The sleeve caps are pleated slightly to ease in the fullness. The pleating was done while the garment was fitted on the body. After the fullness was eased and pleated, the edges were covered with the robings. Inside, the raw edges of the armscye are not turned under or otherwise finished off.

Sleeve Trim: The sleeves end in triple ruffles that are gathered and sewn to the lined sleeves with running stitches. The top ruffle has an extension that forms a gathered band around the arm above the ruffle.

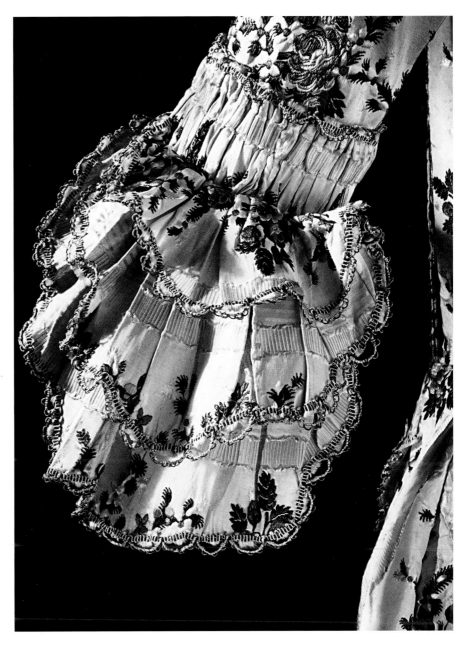

Sleeve ruffles, gathered, scalloped, and edged with looped trim.

What is brocading?

Brocading is a weaving technique that adds extra color and pattern to a textile during the weaving process. Colored or metallic threads are woven as supplementary wefts, in addition to the ground wefts. On the back, one sees that brocading threads are used only where the pattern requires extra color (see photograph on preceeding page). They do not extend from selvage to selvage. This technique conserves expensive materials (using them only where they are seen) and lessens the weight of the textile.

*   This illustration from Diderot's* Encyclopédie *shows small shuttles for each individual color being brocaded into the textile.*

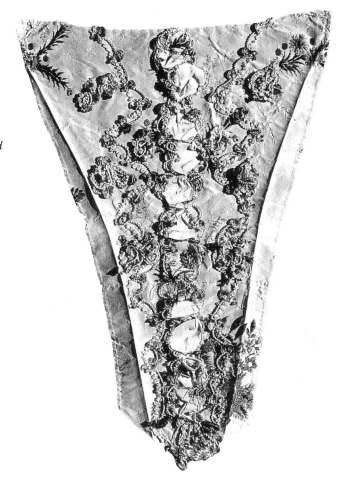

Stomacher, overlaid with fabric puffs and silk fringe.

The upper ruffle was folded lengthwise, gathered, and sewn to the sleeve from the underside of the fold. The middle and lower ruffles were likewise gathered and sewn from the underside. (That is, the ruffles were positioned so that the right side of the ruffle faced the right side of the sleeve while being sewn.) The finished ruffles then fall to cover the stitching. (See illustration, p. 15.)

Gown Skirt: The skirt is shaped to give side width and is sewn to the bodice with only two small pleats to ease the fit. The side shaping was achieved by folding excess fabric to the inside. The excess material was not cut away, making future alterations easier. There are no pocket slits. The front skirt edges are not lined or faced but have narrow hems that are running stitched.

Skirt Trim: The skirt fronts have serpentine bands of self-fabric ruching, averaging 3" (7.6 cm) wide, finished and trimmed by turning the edges under once and topping them with silk loop fringe that is sewn on with running stitch. The ruching was pleated and sewn in place, allowing the pleats to fan out around convex curves. The front skirt edges have looped silk trim.

Polonaise: A ⁵⁄₈" (1.6 cm) button is sewn to the outside of the skirt below the curve of the hip. Positioned on the inside behind each button is a loop of cord for draping the skirt in polonaise style. The skirt can be lifted up in the hand and secured with the cord brought from the back and looped over the button.

Hem: The hem of the gown is faced with thin cream silk, ranging from 7¼" to 9" (18.4 to 22.9 cm) wide, probably because the skirt underside might be seen when draped up.

Stomacher Construction

The stomacher is unlined. All edges are turned under twice and hemmed with running stitch. The puffed fabric trim is not hemmed but is edged with silk fringe sewn loosely in place. There are no hooks for fastening the stomacher. Holes around the edges suggest that it was pinned in place.

About the robe à la Française

The gown with flowing pleats falling from the back shoulders is known to most costume historians as the robe à la Française, *or the gown in the French style. Some people know it as a* Watteau *gown, named after the French painter who recorded women wearing similar fashions. During the eighteenth century, however, English and American women called this style the* sack *or* sacque. *The fashion evolved from a loose negligée gown worn at the French court to a more formal style that was fitted closely to the body at the front. The combination of fitted front and loose back is created by building around the snug bodice lining. Sometimes the lining has interior lacing at the center back, giving adjustability and ease in the bodice beneath the free-flowing pleats.*

Gown from side, drawn
up in polonaise style
using a silk cord looped
over a button.

21

Petticoat Construction

Stitching: The seams are sewn with running stitches and an occasional backstitch using linen thread. All trimming is sewn on with silk thread.

Trim: The petticoat concentrates all of its decoration at the front, where it is seen beneath the gown skirt. The trimming consists of a ruffle cut 10" by 62½" (25.4 by 185.8 cm) and pleated in small box pleats. The ruffle echoes the skirt polonaise by having its own set of ⅝" (1.6 cm) buttons and loops for a sympathetic draped effect. Double bands of 3" (7.6 cm) wide ruching are sewn in serpentine patterns above and below the ruffle.

Lining: Because it is covered by the gown skirt when worn, the back of the petticoat is made of a less expensive textile. This cream-color ribbed silk is backed with plain-woven linen to give it body. The lining extends around the sides and back but not behind the front trimmed panel.

Waistband and Opening: The waistband is a replacement consisting of linen twill tape butted and whipstitched to the pleated skirt. Remnants of an older band made of brocaded silk still survive. The petticoat opens at the side back, not center back. The opening measures 12" (30.5 cm) and is tied at the waist with an extension of the linen twill tape waistband. The raw edges of the opening were finished by folding the silk over the linen backing and sewing with slip stitches. There are no pocket slits in the petticoat.

Hem: The petticoat hem is turned up ¼" (6 mm) and sewn with running stitches. ☝

Petticoat

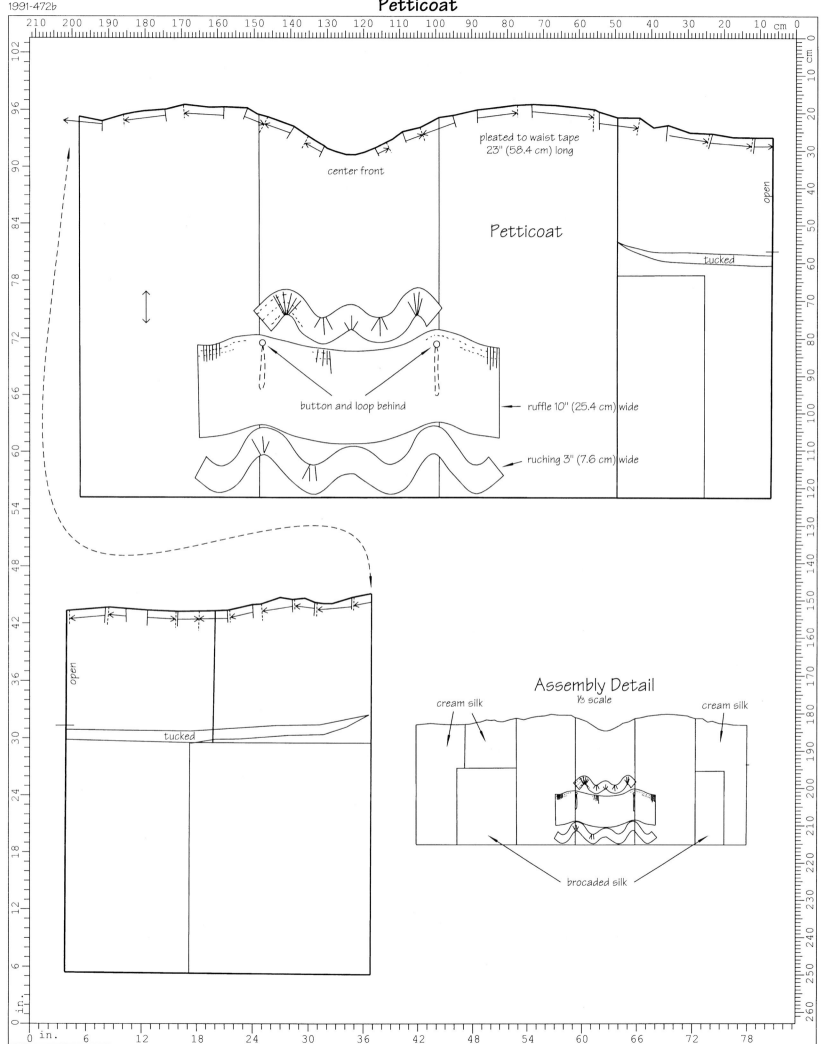

pleated to waist tape
23" (58.4 cm) long

center front

Petticoat

open

tucked

button and loop behind

← ruffle 10" (25.4 cm) wide

← ruching 3" (7.6 cm) wide

open

tucked

Assembly Detail
⅓ scale

cream silk

cream silk

brocaded silk

🌱3

GOWN

England, 1770–1785

Lavender ribbed silk; linen lining; linen tape; silk sewing thread

Overall length, 65" (165.1 cm); back shoulder width, 14" (35.6 cm)
Silk selvage width, 23⅝" (60 cm)
Skirt front length, 39" (99 cm); skirt hem circumference, 117½" (298.5 cm)
Chest, approximately 35" (88.9 cm); waist, approximately 28" (71.1 cm)

Accession number: 1983-233

Silk taffeta gown, shown with skirt drawn up in polonaise style over quilted petticoat no. 4.

Opposite: Gown back. *The back bodice pleats were cut in one with the skirt and released into the skirt fullness.*

By the late 1760s and 1770s, neoclassicism in the other arts had also affected clothing. Gown materials became less heavy, and clothing styles took advantage of lightness in both fabric and color. Elaborate stomacher fronts were often replaced by bodices that pinned or hooked edge to edge at the center front. Skirt pleats became smaller to complement the delicacy of the materials. Many of the new-fashioned gowns had skirts drawn up in puffs using a variety of methods, suggestive of the tucked-up skirts of the dairy maid. This gown of thin lavender silk with pinked trim still retains the tapes for drawing up the skirt in polonaise fashion. The wonderfully decorative polonaise effect is actually achieved by the simple method of tying two pairs of tapes together.

Materials

The gown is made of ribbed silk with a crisp finish. The bodice and sleeves are lined with two different weights of plain-woven linen. The polonaise tapes on the skirt are plain-woven linen. The sewing threads are lavender-color and pink silk.

Change over Time

The lavender-color silk has faded to pink. The sleeves have been narrowed, and darts that once shaped the sleeves at the crook of the arm have been removed. One polonaise tape has been replaced with braided linen tape. Later repairs to the bodice and hem were made with pink sewing silk.

Construction

Stitching: The gown skirt was sewn with 9 running stitches per inch (2.5 cm). Bodice and sleeve seams were lapped and backstitched. Closely spaced backstitches were used in the armscye, where extra strength was needed under the arms.

Bodice: The bodice is styled to be pinned edge to edge at the center front. Because there are no darts or stomacher, the bodice achieves its shaping through the center back and side seams and through pleats that taper toward the waist in the back. The bodice back pleats were cut in one with the skirt, laid in place over the lining, and sewn down with running stitches. The pleats are released into the skirt at the center back, below the natural waist. This style is called *en fourreau*, or the *English back*.

The center back seam was sewn with backstitch and trimmed close to the stitching, leaving seam allowances approximately ⅜" (1 cm) wide. This seam is hidden by the lining. The bodice seams curve from the underarm to the hip, further shaping the bodice. To form these seams, the bodice front pieces were lapped over the bodice back and sewn from the top with backstitches through the

fashion fabrics. The bodice is lined with white plain-woven linen, brought out to the edges and sewn with running stitches (probably later repairs) and slanted stitches that come through to the front side in places. (See diagram for *point à rabattre* on p. 8.) The center back seam of the bodice lining is stitched with backstitches; the other two curved lining seams are turned under and sewn with slanted hemming stitches, not worked through to the front.

Neckline Finishing: The back neck is bound with a shaped and folded piece of silk positioned between the shoulder bands, turned under, and stitched. It is largely hidden by the trimming stitched over the top. In contrast to most earlier gowns, the interior finish of this example is very neatly done.

Bodice and Sleeve Trim: The neckline and sleeves are trimmed with strips of self-fabric, about two times fullness, pinked in scallops, tucked, and running stitched in place. The pinked edges are otherwise unfinished. Pinking is described on page 14.

Sleeves: The sleeves are cut on the cross grain of the fabric, with the warps running around the arm instead of lengthwise. They are lined with two different linens, pieced together and following the pattern of the sleeves. The sleeve seams are lapped and sewn with running- and spaced backstitches through both the fashion fabric and lining, leaving very wide seam allowances of 1" to 1½" (2.54 to 3.8 cm). (See diagram, p. 8.) The arm openings were finished by bringing the linen lining down to the edge, turning the raw edges of the linen and silk in toward each other, and stitching the two together with running stitches. These running stitches are hidden by the sleeve trim. The lined sleeves are partially set into the lined bodice using closely spaced backstitches, leaving the sleeve cap free to be fitted directly on the body. The cap was pleated to fit the wearer's shoulder and held in place with the shoulder band, which was laid over and secured with running stitches all around. Similarly, the raw edges of the linen shoulder band lining are turned under and slip-stitched.

Gown, open to show linen lining and tapes used to draw the skirt up in polonaise style.

Gown

Bodice Back Lining
stitch lines
center back

Neck Trim
approximately 68" (173 cm) long

Shoulder Band
back

Bodice Trim Sketch
(enlarged)
front
back

Bodice Front
stitch line of trim
sleeve seam
center front
skirt sewn here

Shoulder Band Lining
back

Back Neck Binding
fold

Bodice Front Lining
center front

Sleeve
back
tucks at top of arm
front
tucks

Sleeve Trim
approximately 24" (61 cm) long

neck binding sewn here
center back
pleat

Skirt and Bodice Back
folded back
pleat direction ¼" (6 mm) pleats
pleated from here
tape tie
skirt front
selvage seam
selvage seam
tape tie
fold

Skirt: The pleated skirt is made from 5 panels of silk, seamed at the selvages with 9 running stitches per inch (2.5 cm), leaving seam allowances of ⅛" (3 mm). There are no pocket slits. The skirt is stitched to the bodice beginning about 4½" (11.4 cm) from the center front point. Excess length of the skirt front is folded back at the dip of the waist and pleated, not cut off. This technique permitted easier alterations in the future. The ¼" (6 mm) pleats of the skirt waist are directed toward the center back. On the underside, each pleat is caught by a stitch carried from pleat to pleat. The

unlined skirt is open at the front to show a petticoat worn beneath. The skirt fronts were hemmed by turning selvages under ⅛" (3 mm) and stitching them with running stitches.

Polonaise: The polonaise effect is achieved through two pairs of tape stitched to the back side of the skirt. To draw up the skirt, the tapes are brought together and tied. The skirt can be worn without being drawn up simply by releasing the ties.

Hem: The original hem, now restitched in places, was ⅛" (3 mm) wide, sewn with running stitch.

Gown interior showing the center back seam and a portion of the armscye. The skirt pleats are caught with stitches on the back side. The linen tapes, tied in a bow, draw the skirt up in polonaise.

4
PETTICOAT

England, 1750–1775

Pink silk satin; white glazed worsted backing (*tammy*); pink woolen batting; pink silk ribbon hem binding; pink silk quilting thread; linen tape waistband

Skirt front length, 35" (88.9 cm); waist (altered), 24" (61 cm); skirt hem circumference, 96" (243.8 cm)
Satin selvage width, approximately 17" (43.2 cm); worsted selvage width, approximately 28½" (72.4 cm)

Accession number: 1953-436

Although many eighteenth-century gowns had matching petticoats, quilted petticoats offered variety to a woman's wardrobe. A gown could be worn with its matching petticoat or with a contrasting one for a change of color or appearance. With their fluffy wool batting, quilted petticoats also gave extra warmth in cold rooms or for winter wear. Petticoats were often made by professional quilters in England and exported as ready-made items to the American colonies. This supposition is borne out not only in the written records but in the surviving objects themselves. Many petticoats in museum collections share similarities of design and material that suggest a single workshop or quilter. These similarities include the use of very soft satin for the face and glazed worsted for the backing. The petticoat shown here is related in design to several others in Colonial Williamsburg's collection. All have the same spiky quality in the flowers and swags. In eighteenth-century records, quilted petticoats are often called *quilts* or *wearing quilts,* not to be confused with those for beds.

Materials

The face of the petticoat is made from pink silk satin seamed in pieces approximately 17" (43.2 cm) wide. (The quilting draws in the textiles, so it is difficult to determine the exact selvage width.) It is quilted with pink silk thread through woolen batting. The batting was dyed pink so as not to show through the thin silk on the right side. The backing fabric is white worsted, woven in plain weave 28½" (72.4 cm) wide and glazed after weaving. This is probably the fabric called *tammy* in the eighteenth century. There is an even pattern of holes in the woolen selvages, resulting from the textile's having been stretched on tenterhooks during the manufacturing process. The hem binding is a 1⅜" (3.5 cm) wide ribbed silk ribbon.

Change over Time

The original pink color has faded to beige in large areas. The waistband and hem binding are replacements. The alterations probably occurred around

Front view of silk satin petticoat, quilted to wool backing.

1840, when full skirts and quilted petticoats returned to fashion.

Construction

Stitching: The petticoat is constructed and quilted with running stitches. The seams of the satin were sewn with right sides together. The seams of the backing are overlapped at the selvages and sewn.

Quilting: The petticoat was quilted as a flat rectangle. The satin face was seamed to the desired size, then layered with fluffy woolen batting between it and the prepared backing of glazed wool. The batting extends only as far up as the quilted design, not to the waistband, thus eliminating excessive bulk at the waist. The quilting is worked in pink silk with 10 to 15 running stitches to the inch (2.5 cm).

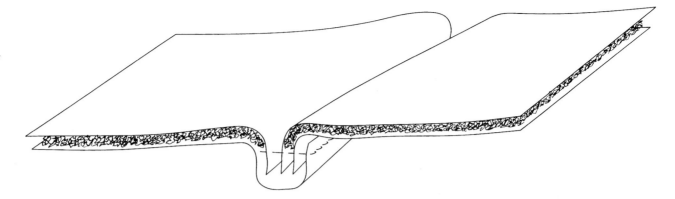

Method of sewing the center back seam. The raw edges are bound with an extension of the wool backing.

Waist and Opening: The skirt has extra length over the hips to accommodate modest side hoops. The extra length was added at the top, not at the hem. The skirt does not retain its original pleating pattern because the waistband has been replaced. The present skirt treatment consists of a wide box pleat at center front. The remainder of the fullness is gathered up in deep cartridge pleats, caught to the ¾" (1.9 cm) linen tape waistband at the front of each pleat. It is not known what the original waist treatment was. The replacement waistband ties at center back, similar to the skirts of some dresses from 1840. This probably was an early alteration to allow the petticoat to be reused. The center back opening was finished by folding the selvages of the silk satin over the raw edges and stitching them to the backing with running stitches worked through all layers. There are no pocket slits. The center back seam is sewn with running stitches. The raw edges of the seam are encased in an extension of the wool lining (see sketch above).

Hem: The hem at the bottom of the skirt is faced with ribbed silk ribbon, approximately 1⅜" (3.5 cm) wide, replaced from an earlier hem binding. The ribbon is sewn to the right side of the skirt with about ⅛" (3 mm) showing on the right side of the petticoat, and the remainder is folded to the inside and sewn with running stitches. ☙

Petticoat turned inside out, showing the waistband and back opening. Note the skirt with cartridge pleats, the shiny texture of the glazed wool tammy backing, the overlapping tammy seam, and the edge finish of the placket opening. The waistband and cartridge pleat treatment date from the nineteenth century.

1953-436

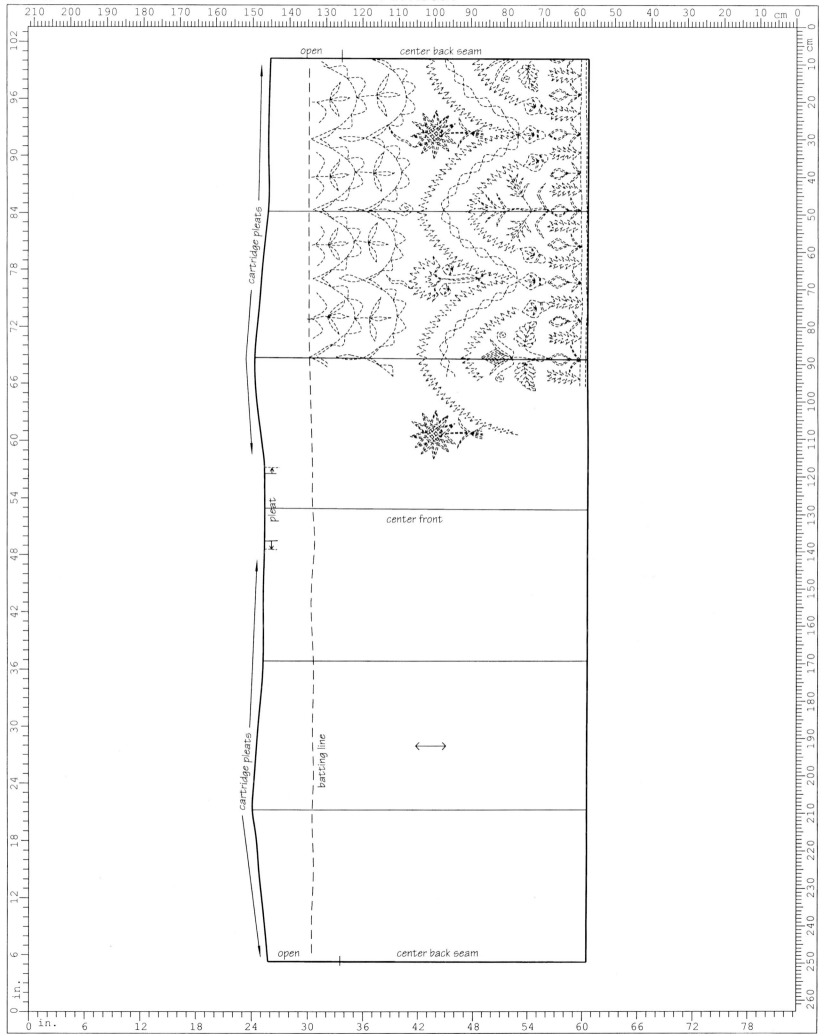

Petticoat Quilting Pattern
quilted with 11 to 15 running stitches per inch (2.5 cm)

More about glazed wool

Glazed worsted textiles are fascinating examples of a sophisticated manufacturing technique. Wool takes on a high gloss when subjected to pressure and heat. Eighteenth-century manufacturers deliberately utilized this property to create shiny wool textiles by folding the woven yardage and placing it in a press. The Press for Glazing Stuffs is from a 1748 text and shows how stacks of wool textiles were compressed and flattened. On the table at the right are pasteboards used to separate the folded layers. The pasteboards were used along with heated plates between the folds of the textile.

The Press for Glazing Stuffs.

Petticoat turned inside out to show the permanent creases in the glazed backing. Such creases are valuable evidence of the original manufacturing technique and should not be pressed flat or removed.

5

PETTICOAT

England, 1750–1775

Cream silk satin; cream glazed worsted backing; undyed woolen batting; silk quilting thread; linen piecing

Skirt front length, 37" (94 cm); waist (altered), 27½" (69.9 cm); hem circumference, 100½" (255.3 cm)
Satin selvage width, about 17½" (44.5 cm); worsted selvage width, about 27½" (69.9 cm)

Accession number: 1985-118

Front view of quilted silk petticoat.

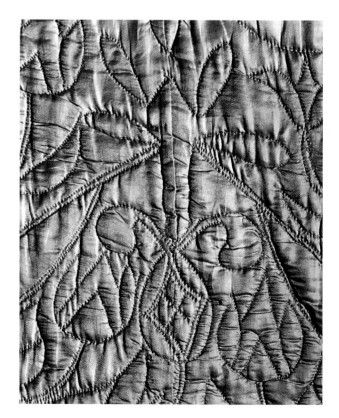

Right: *Detail of quilting with vertical piecing seam visible in the center.*

This petticoat shares many of the features of petticoat number 4. It was quilted by a professional, and its backing fabric is permanently creased from the glazing process. The lower half of the quilted design features multiple swags of various widths, filled with dense flowers, leaves, and zigzags. The upper portion has a filling of lively flowers swimming from left to the right.

Materials

The petticoat is made of cream-colored silk satin with a very soft texture. The satin is in panels approximately 17½" (44.5 cm) wide. (The quilting draws in the textile, making an exact measurement impossible.) The backing is cream-color glazed worsted woven in plain weave approximately 27½"

(69.9 cm) wide. The selvages still retain an even pattern of holes from tenterhooks. The batting is natural-color woolen fiber. A narrow strip of linen is used as a backing at the top of the petticoat where alterations have occurred. The present (replaced) waistband is silk ribbon 2½" (6.4 cm) wide, folded lengthwise.

Change over Time

Approximately 2" (5 cm) of the petticoat's top has been replaced. The replaced section is made of ribbed silk or a wide ribbon, backed with linen, without any batting or quilting stitches. The waist has been repleated onto a new waistband. The petticoat's vertical seam is now positioned to the right of center front, suggesting that the petticoat was turned around from back to front when the top was replaced and repleated. The hem and waistband have been repaired with modern material.

Petticoat Quilting Pattern

quilted with 12 to 16 running stitches per inch (2.5 cm)

Petticoat

pleated

center back

pleated

batting line

open

center front

open

seam

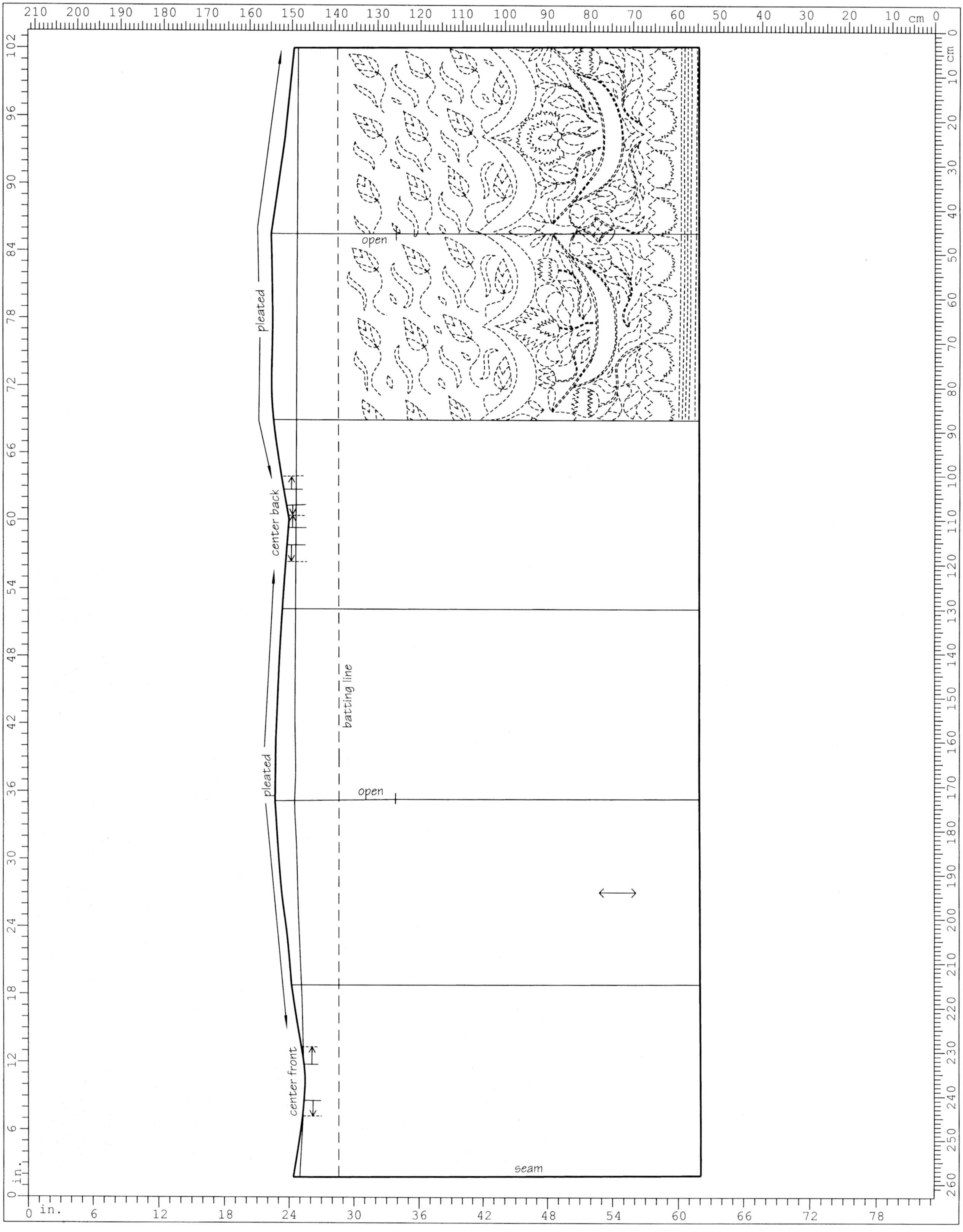

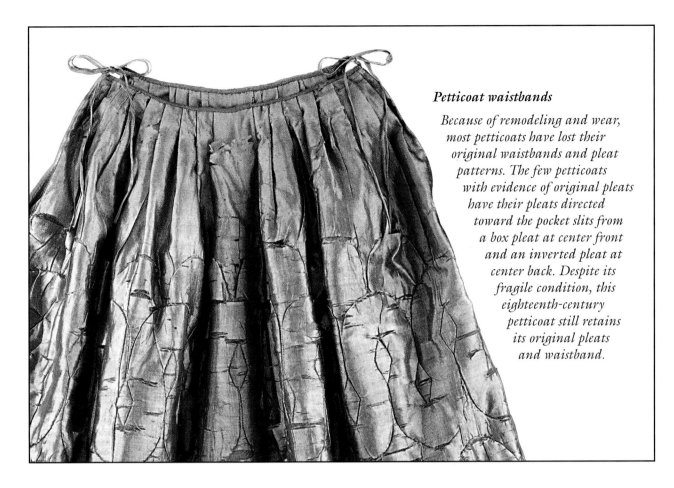

Petticoat waistbands

Because of remodeling and wear, most petticoats have lost their original waistbands and pleat patterns. The few petticoats with evidence of original pleats have their pleats directed toward the pocket slits from a box pleat at center front and an inverted pleat at center back. Despite its fragile condition, this eighteenth-century petticoat still retains its original pleats and waistband.

Side opening showing the replaced waistband and later extension at the top. The pocket slit was finished by folding the silk selvages over the raw edges of the worsted backing material.

Construction

Stitching: The petticoat is quilted and constructed with running stitches.

Quilting: This petticoat was quilted in the same manner as number 4. The satin was seamed to the desired size, assembled with the batting and backing, and quilted as a flat piece. The quilting is worked in cream silk with 12 to 16 running stitches to the inch (2.5 cm). As is true of the other petticoat, the batting extends only as far as the quilting.

Waist and Opening: Two side slits form the waist opening and give access to the pockets. The pocket slits are positioned at the selvages of the satin. The cut raw edges of batting and backing were bound by folding the extended satin selvages over the layers and stitching with running stitches on the reverse. The front pleat pattern is a center box pleat with the remaining pleats directed toward the pocket slits on either side; the back pleats are directed toward the sides from a pair of box pleats at center back.

Vertical Seam: The vertical seam, repositioned off-center at the front, was sewn with right sides together using running stitches through all layers; the raw edges were felled (turned under and stitched down to the petticoat).

Hem: The raw edges of the silk and the tammy were turned inside toward each other and stitched with running stitches. 🌱

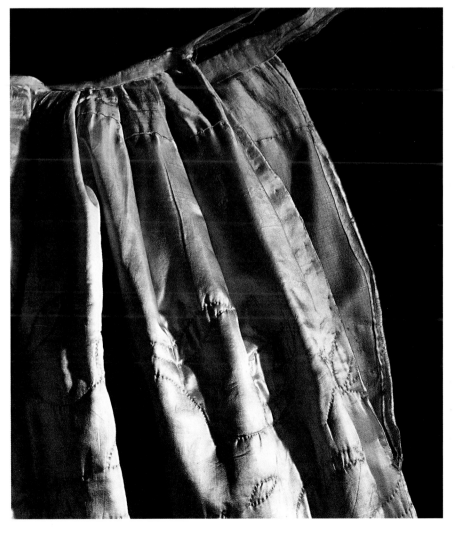

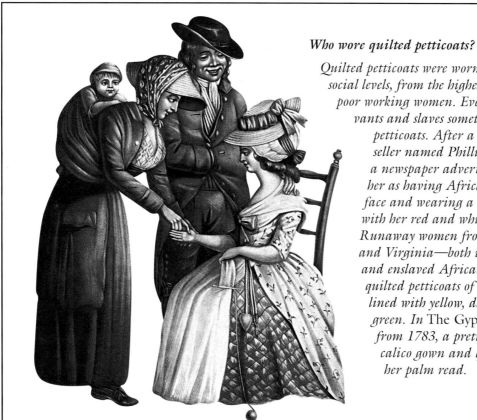

Who wore quilted petticoats?

Quilted petticoats were worn by women of all social levels, from the highest ranks of society to poor working women. Even indentured servants and slaves sometimes had quilted petticoats. After a Charleston oyster seller named Phillis ran away in 1776, a newspaper advertisement described her as having African markings on her face and wearing a black quilted "coat" with her red and white "callico" gown. Runaway women from South Carolina and Virginia—both indentured whites and enslaved African-Americans—wore quilted petticoats of black, red, blue, blue lined with yellow, dark brown, and green. In The Gypsie Fortune-Teller *from 1783, a pretty country girl in a calico gown and quilted petticoat has her palm read.*

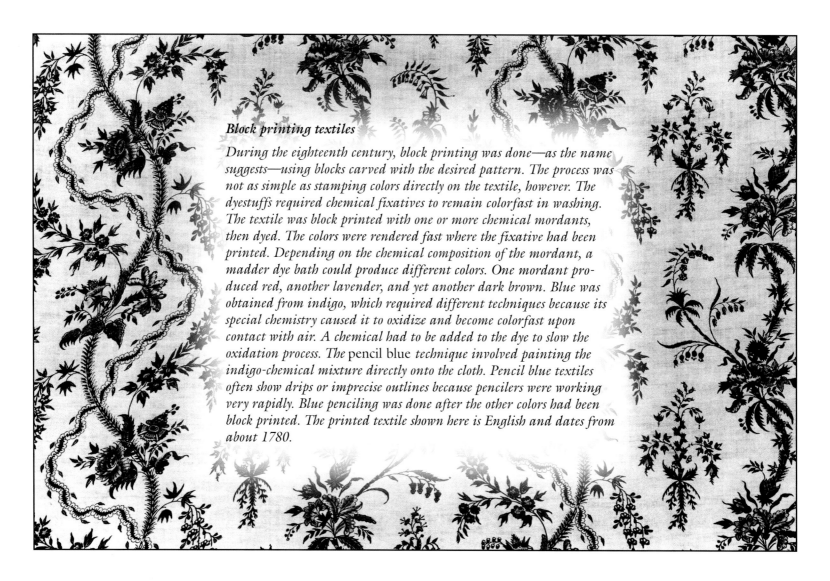

Block printing textiles

During the eighteenth century, block printing was done—as the name suggests—using blocks carved with the desired pattern. The process was not as simple as stamping colors directly on the textile, however. The dyestuffs required chemical fixatives to remain colorfast in washing. The textile was block printed with one or more chemical mordants, then dyed. The colors were rendered fast where the fixative had been printed. Depending on the chemical composition of the mordant, a madder dye bath could produce different colors. One mordant produced red, another lavender, and yet another dark brown. Blue was obtained from indigo, which required different techniques because its special chemistry caused it to oxidize and become colorfast upon contact with air. A chemical had to be added to the dye to slow the oxidation process. The pencil blue *technique involved painting the indigo-chemical mixture directly onto the cloth. Pencil blue textiles often show drips or imprecise outlines because pencilers were working very rapidly. Blue penciling was done after the other colors had been block printed. The printed textile shown here is English and dates from about 1780.*

JACKET

France, 1775–1785

Block-printed cotton with pencil blue; plain-woven linen linings; replaced silk trim; linen sewing thread

Length, 22" (55.9 cm); back shoulder width, 12" (30.4 cm); chest, 30½" (77.5 cm); waist, 23" (58.4 cm)

Accession number: 1962-259

Jackets came in a variety of styles. The fronts of some had stomachers, whereas others laced shut or buttoned edge to edge at the front. Sleeves sometimes had cuffs. This jacket was laced over a triangular stomacher, now missing; it could also have been worn with a large kerchief that filled in and expanded the front. Although this jacket and the one illustrated on page 42 are French, similar jackets were worn in England and America.

Materials

This jacket is made of plain-woven cotton, printed with madder colors using wood blocks (see p. 38). The blue is brushed on separately in the technique called *pencil blue.* The sewing threads are linen, the thickest used for overcasting the eyelets. Two different linens, pieced together, line the jacket. An

unknown material, probably linen, is used as front interfacing to support the eyelets.

Change over Time

The trim at the opening of the sleeves has been replaced with modern silk gimp. Because of shrinkage and the stress of lacing the jacket tightly, the center back lining seam has opened.

Construction

Stitching: The jacket is sewn with backstitches, slip stitches, whipstitches, and slanted hemming stitches. The eyelets are overcast. The textile was pieced with backstitches and whipstitches.

Lining: The jacket is fully lined with two different qualities of linen. The upper body lining is white linen; that of the tails is darker linen. Unlike modern clothing construction, the lining was not constructed separately and sewn into the garment at the end. Rather, each section was lined individually and the two were then treated as one piece. The garment seams are stitched in the manner of the sketch below. That is to say, the two printed decorative pieces and one of the linings were sewn from the top in one operation with backstitches that went through all three fabrics. Next, the raw edges of the unstitched lining were turned under and slipstitched over the previous seam.

Left: *Printed cotton jacket shown from the back with a blue quilted silk petticoat of the same period.*

Below: *Construction of jacket seams.*

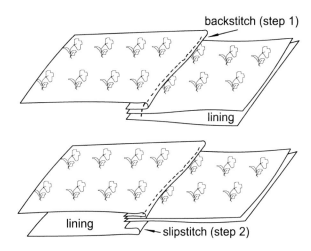

Bodice Shaping: The bodice is shaped without bust darts. The skirts are designed to flare over the hips and petticoat with great economy of cut and construction. The tails were cut as part of the main garment pieces. Further shaping was achieved with slashes at the front waist. The slashes are bound with printed self-fabric, cut on the straight grain.

Sleeves: Each sleeve has a single seam positioned at the front of the arm and ending at the crook of the elbow. The sleeve seam meets the bodice front approximately 1" (2.5 cm) below the horizontal seam that joins the shoulder piece to the bodice front. The sleeves were shaped to cup over the elbows by sewing a long, curving dart below the elbow and trimming away the excess fabric. The dart was lapped and backstitched from the top through the folded layers. This method contrasts with modern techniques, in which darts are folded with right sides together and stitched. The lined and finished sleeves are set into the armscye with backstitches worked from the outside, going through all layers except the bodice lining. The bodice lining's raw edges were turned under and roughly stitched to cover the raw edges of the sleeve and armscye.

Closure: The jacket is laced at the front through a series of eyelets. The eyelets are worked with overcast stitches through all layers—printed decorative fabric, interfacing, and lining. The heavy linen stitching thread is carried from eyelet to eyelet on the back.

Interfacing: The front is interfaced with two strips of fabric cut about 1⅝" (4.1 cm) wide. The interfacing supports and stiffens the front closure.

Edge Finishing and Hem: No facings are used in the jacket. The linings were brought to the outside edges, where both the printed cotton and the lining were turned under and sewn with small stitches that caught the lining and printed fabric in one, giving the appearance of slanted hemming stitches from the lining side and running stitches from the top (*point à rabattre sous la main;* see p. 8). This treatment continued to form the bottom hems. A second row of stitches was worked in running stitches about ¼" (6 mm) from the neck edge.

On the left are the front eyelets. The center back seam of the pieced linen lining is to the right.

Jacket

Sketch of Back

Sleeve

cap

back

front

underarm

crook of arm

Shoulder Piece

arm opening

arm opening

elbow

seamed

sleeve seam

Bodice Back

center back seam

Interfacing

Bodice Front
(two pieces)

open

bound slash

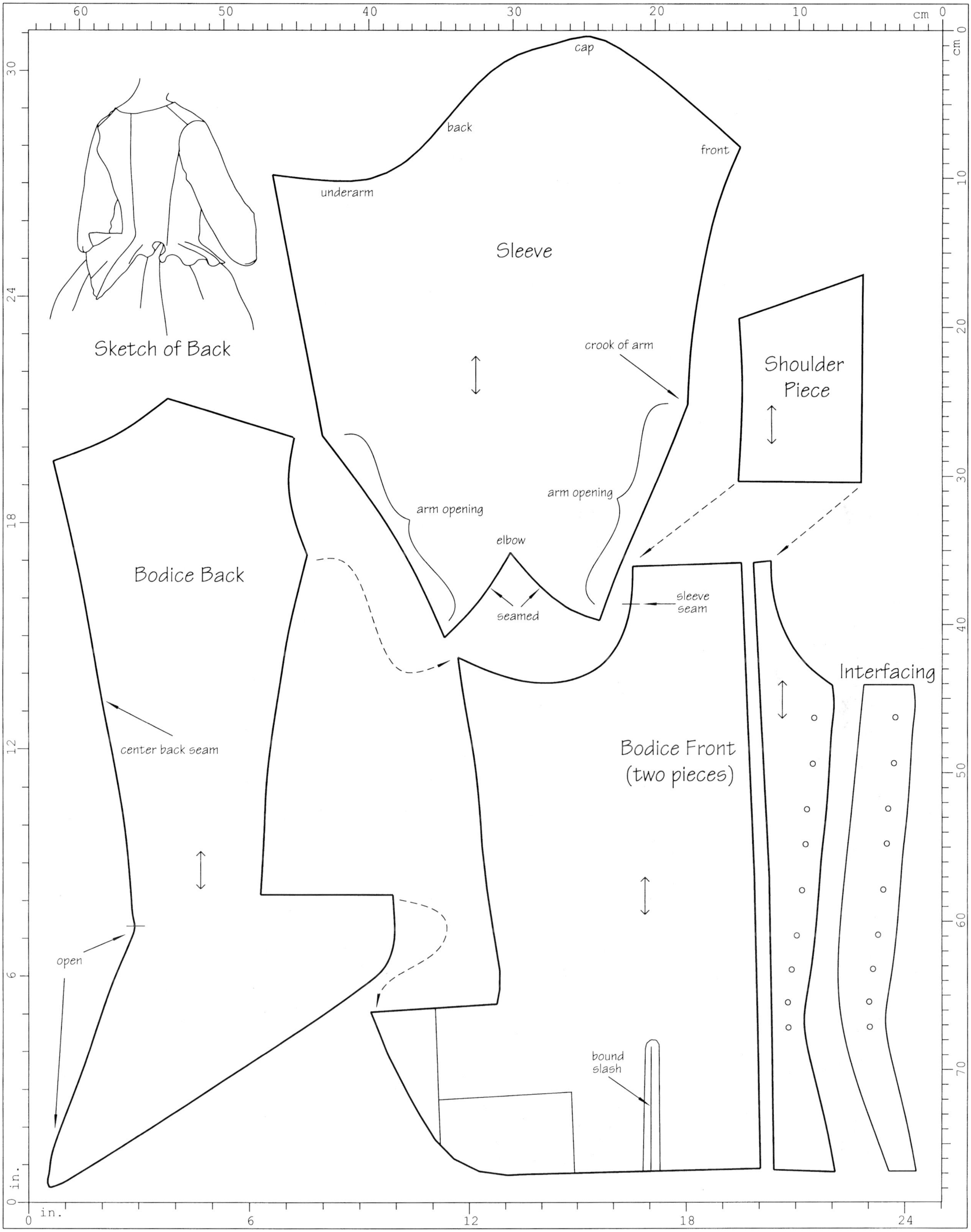

Jacket shown open. It has a full lining consisting of two different linen textiles that are brought out to the edges and stitched to the printed textile.

Who wore jackets?

Fitted jackets worn with separate petticoats were practical and comfortable for work and informal occasions. They were more economical than gowns because they did not have full overskirts requiring yards of fabric. They were daytime wear for women of many social levels. Virginia plantation owners issued woolen jackets and petticoats to slave women working in the fields during the eighteenth century. A slave woman from Frederick County, Maryland, was wearing a "Callico Jacket without Cuffs, and a Callico Petticoat, the fore Part Patch-Work," when she ran away in 1770. The woman in the French engraving to the left wears a jacket laced over a stomacher and a neck handkerchief filling in the low neckline. The illustration at right is taken from Diderot's Encyclopédie.

7

Short Gown

Textiles printed in England; gown worn in America, 1775–1815

Plain-woven cotton, block-printed in madder colors; linen tape; linen sewing thread

Overall length, 28½" (72.4 cm); chest, 31" (78.7 cm); waist, 31½" (80 cm)
Selvage width of textile cannot be determined (at least 27" [68.6 cm])

Accession number: 1985-242

Short gown front, open to show the contrasting printed lining.

An Englishwoman in a 1765 print wears a kerchief, short gown, and patched petticoat.

For physical labor and very informal occasions, women wore short gowns with separate petticoats as comfortable alternatives to fitted gowns with long, full skirts. Constructed to fit loosely and reach about midthigh, short gowns had the advantages of being comfortable and relatively inexpensive, as they required a minimum of fabric. They were shaped as flat pieces and usually constructed without elaborate fitting. When worn, they were pinned at the front and held around the body by the apron strings. These characteristics made short gowns a practical garment for working and pregnant women. A convict servant spinner and dairy maid had a striped "linsey" short gown when she ran away in 1769. The young slave maid who accompanied Thomas Jefferson's daughter to Paris in 1787 had two calico short gowns and petticoats in her wardrobe, along with Irish linen aprons, three pair of stockings, and a shawl handkerchief to wear around her shoulders and neck. (In contrast, Miss Jefferson's wardrobe had no short gowns. She wore fine linen and muslin frock dresses trimmed with lace and blue sashes.)

Short gowns changed very little over time and are difficult to date precisely. From the front, the example shown above appears to date in the 1770s or 1780s, but the back has a drawstring placed above waist level, possibly indicating a date in the early nineteenth century. The drawstring is either intended to provide some shaping at the back or is a nod to later fashions, when waistlines rose above the natural waist. This is a very small garment that may have been worn by a young girl.

Materials

This short gown is made of two different block-printed cottons. The outer fabric was originally white printed with red, purple, brown, and pencil blue. The lining is printed with a floral design, originally purple or brown on white. The seams are stitched with linen. Linen tape forms the adjustment drawstrings at the back neck and shoulders.

Change over Time

The garment is exceptionally fragile. The iron in the mordant used for the printing process has caused some colors to darken to brown and etch through the cotton ground. (See p. 38 for a discussion of block printing.) Purple is especially vulnerable to change over time, seldom surviving in its original hue because of the long-term effects of its mordant. The lining was probably purple on white but is now brown on beige. A small patch of a different floral-printed cotton is at the center front hem and is probably a later repair.

Construction

Stitching: The gown was sewn with backstitches, running stitches, and slip stitches. The seams were sewn with linen in both back- and running stitches.

Cut: The short gown was cut very simply from a length of fabric and shaped with cutouts under the arms, a hole for the neck, and a slash down the front for an opening. Triangles taken from the arm cutouts were moved down to complete the sweep at the hem. Both the garment and lining were pieced to save fabric.

Sleeves: The sleeves were cut in one piece with the body of the gown. The sleeves are extended by rectangles intended to be turned up in cuffs 2" to 3" (5 to 7.6 cm) wide. The cuffs are constructed of the primary floral pattern. They are folded to the inside and pieced with scraps of both the front and lining fabrics.

Drawstrings: There are linen tape drawstrings at the back neck. Each tape is tacked at the shoulder and runs in a channel formed between the primary fabric and the lining; the drawstrings protrude from a center back interior eyelet for adjustment. A second adjustment tape runs in a stitched channel about 6½" (16.5 cm) down from the shoulders on the back of the gown. The drawstrings provided some shaping for the otherwise unfitted garment.

Lining and Edge Finishing: There is a full lining of printed cotton, cut to the same size and shape as

The back neckline of the short gown has linen tape drawstrings emerging from a center back eyelet. The center front was pinned closed.

1985-242

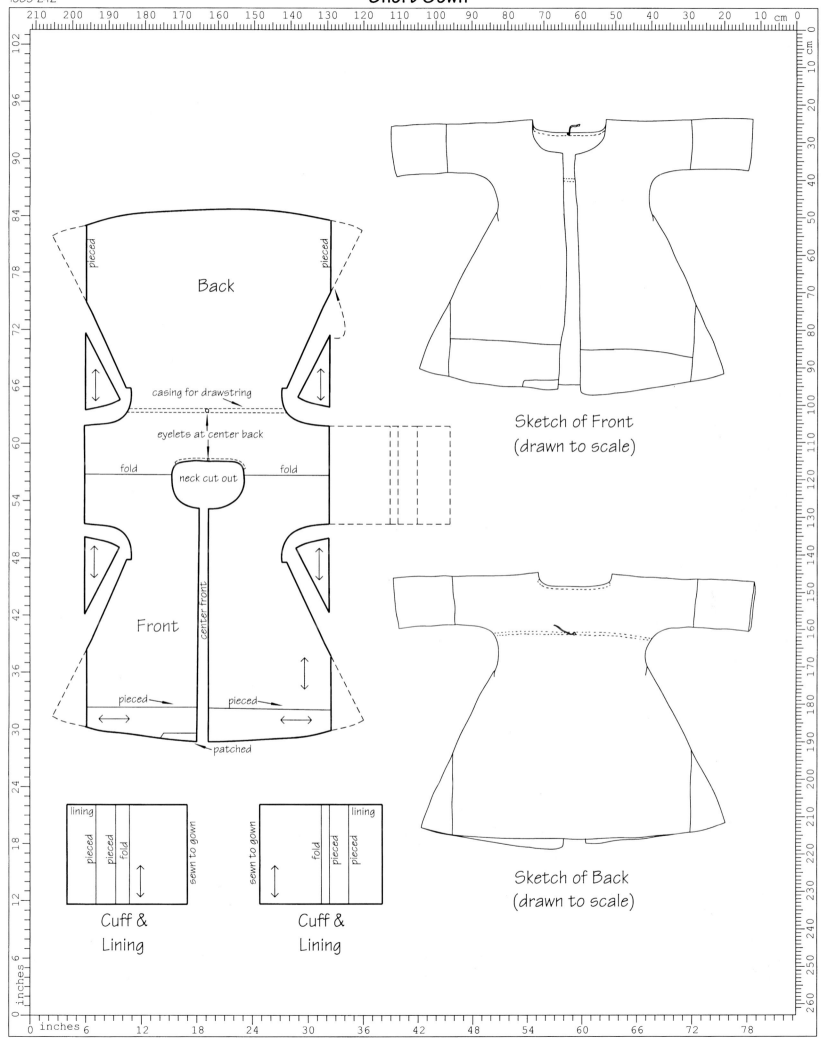

Back

pieced

pieced

casing for drawstring

eyelets at center back

fold

neck cut out

fold

center front

Front

pieced

pieced

patched

Sketch of Front
(drawn to scale)

Sketch of Back
(drawn to scale)

lining

pieced

pieced

fold

sewn to gown

Cuff &
Lining

sewn to gown

fold

pieced

pieced

lining

Cuff &
Lining

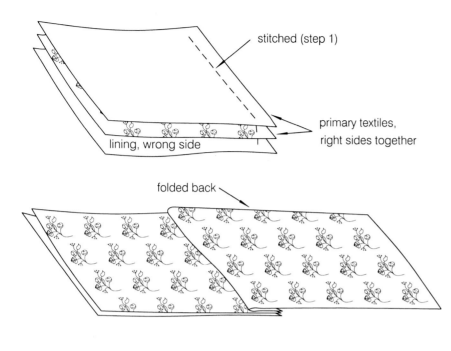

stitched (step 1)

primary textiles, right sides together

lining, wrong side

folded back

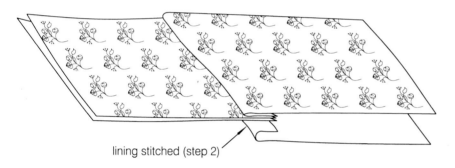

lining stitched (step 2)

Stitching technique used on the side seams.

the outer garment. All of the raw edges—hem, center front slash, and neck—were turned to the inside and slip-stitched to the lining at the edges.

Side Seams: Each side seam was sewn in two operations. First, the two fashion fabrics were placed with right sides together. Next, the wrong side of one lining piece was placed against the wrong side of fashion fabric. The three textiles were backstitched. The remaining lining was brought up to the seam, turned under, and stitched down to cover all the raw edges. (See sketch at left.) A pair of tucks worked into each side seam at waist level gives a little extra fullness over the hips. The tucks measure about $1/4"$ (6 mm) deep and form an inverted box pleat. Each pleat is reinforced with a thread tack at the top.

Hem: The hem was turned under and enclosed with the lining as described in the section on lining and edge finishing. ☙

8

APRON

France, 1770–1785

Plain-woven cotton, block printed in madder colors of red, purple, and brown with pencil blue; linen sewing threads

Overall length, 41¼" (104.8 cm); skirt length at center front, 29¼" (74.3 cm)
Selvage width, 37¼" (96.6 cm)

Accession number: 1952-67

Aprons were not just for cleanliness and protection while working. Many eighteenth-century aprons were decorative and elaborate fashion accessories, made of fine cotton or silk and embellished with needlework or printing. Because of its washable but decorative fabric, this apron probably functioned as both accessory and protection. It has an attached bib but no straps to tie it in place around the neck; the bib was pinned directly to the wearer's clothing using straight pins. (Safety pins were not invented until the nineteenth century.) The bib has repair patches at the corners, attesting to the wear caused by repeated pinning. Today this style of apron is sometimes called a *pinner* or *pinafore*. In the eighteenth century, however, the term *pinner* usually meant a woman's cap or

headdress with long flaps that were pinned up. By the nineteenth century, bib aprons were referred to as *pinners*. The apron's waist comes to a deep point at the center front, conforming to the style of many gowns that had pointed center front waistlines. The ties on eighteenth-century aprons were typically narrow tapes or ribbons—apron strings—not wide sashes.

Materials

This apron is constructed of plain-woven cotton, block printed in madder colors with the addition of pencil blue. (For a discussion of block printing, see p. 38.) There are no linings. The original sewing thread was linen. Cotton thread has been used for later repairs.

More about apron materials

Eighteenth-century aprons came in a variety of materials. Surviving aprons are made of silk taffeta embroidered with colored silks and metal threads, fine white sheer cottons or linens embroidered with white or colored linen, and white sheer cotton checked with heavy white threads woven in at intervals. Milliners in Williamsburg, Virginia, advertised that they had for sale "spotted, needle worked, black and white silk, worked muslin, black patent net, and lawn" aprons. Silk or embroidered cotton aprons were worn as decorative accessories with a dressy gown. They were the products of professional needleworkers. More commonly, everyday work aprons were made of coarse, sturdy linen. Work aprons were plain white, checked, or striped linen. The newspaper notices of runaway servant women often describe their clothing; many of these women had checked aprons. The apron at right, made of silk and embroidered with metal threads, is European and dates 1730 to 1750.

Left: *Block-printed apron shown with silk gown and reproduction ruffles. The gown is probably French and dates 1770 to 1785.*

Change over Time

The bib is distorted and shows some wear, both from the pins originally used to fasten it in place and from abrasion and creasing at the waist. The bib is now lined with modern conservation support fabric and is mended. The skirt has about ⅝" (1.6 cm) of fabric trimmed off the left edge, almost to the waistband, and has been rehemmed using modern cotton thread.

Construction

Stitching: The apron was sewn with backstitches, whipstitches, and slanted hemming stitches. Both the bib and the skirt were originally unlined and simple in their construction.

Skirt: The skirt is made from two widths of printed cotton, seamed vertically. The seam is positioned just off the center point. This long seam was backstitched with linen and pressed open; because of the presence of selvages, it is otherwise unfinished. A selvage finishes the proper right edge of the skirt. The left edge has been cut parallel to the selvage and is hemmed with modern cotton. The material cut from the skirt was used as repair patches,

probably in the twentieth century. The skirt is gathered to a narrow self-fabric waistband and dips to a point at the center front.

Waist: The waistband is made from a fabric strip cut on the straight grain and folded over the gathered skirt material to encase the raw edges. The raw edges of the waistband were turned inside and hemmed with slanted hemming stitches. The finished waistband measures about ¼" (6 mm) wide. The original waist ties are missing at the sides, but buttonhole-stitch loops, probably replacements, are sewn at the ends of the waistband for attaching ties of ribbon or tape.

Bib: The bib was pieced from three fragments. The piecing seams are backstitched and felled. All edges of the bib are hemmed. During construction the bib was completed and hemmed all around, then butted to the completed skirt and whipstitched edge to edge to join the two pieces.

Hem: Characteristic of most eighteenth-century sewing, the hems do not waste any fabric but measure a mere ⅛" to ¼" (3 to 6 mm) wide. The hem was sewn with slanted hemming stitches. ✿

Apron

sewn to bib

gathered into 9¼"
(23.5 cm)

center front

Left Skirt

Bib

pieced

patched

gathered into 9¼"
(23.5 cm)

sewn to bib

Waistband

½" × 18½" long
(1.2 x 47 cm)

Right Skirt

center front

Idealized Version of Apron

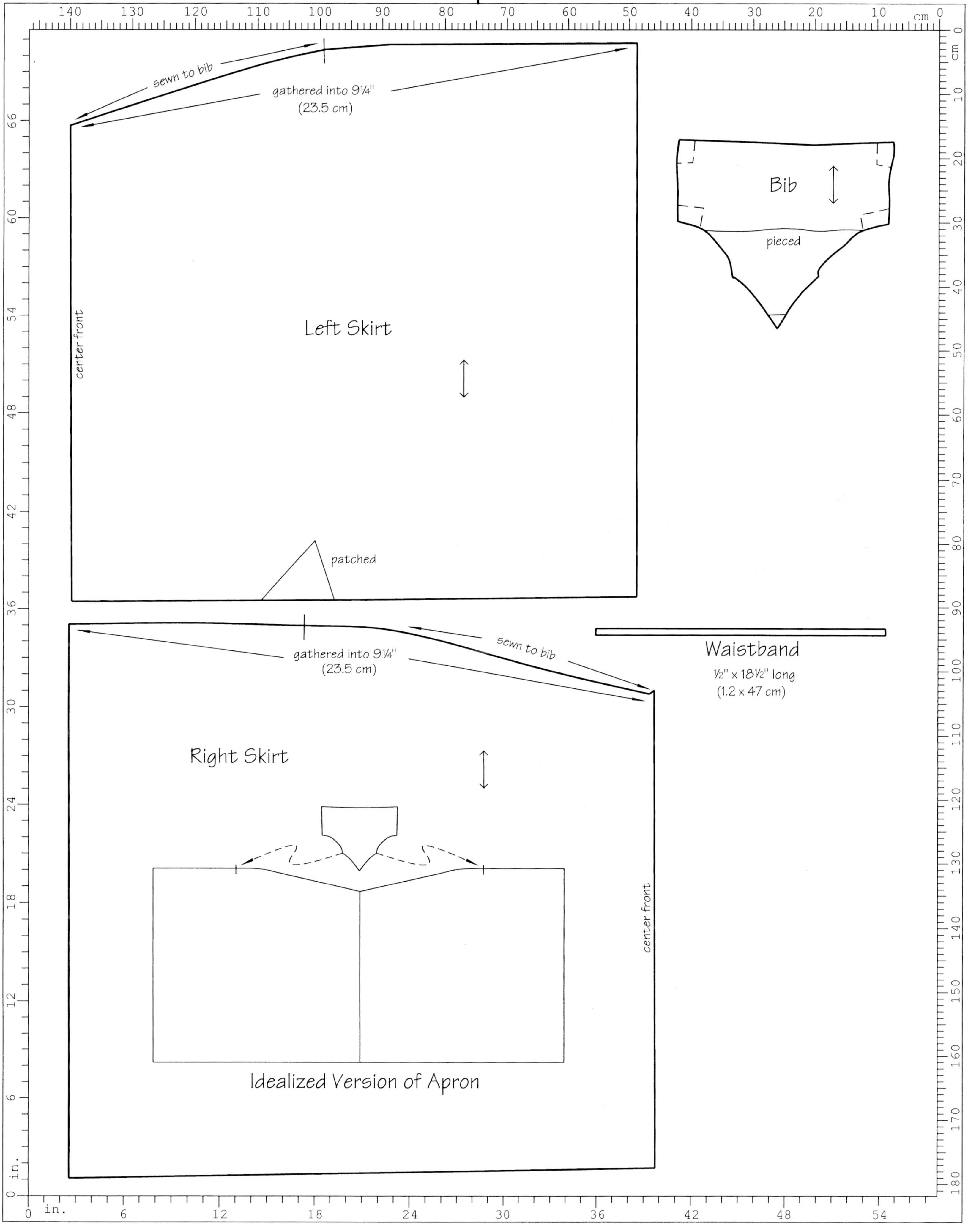

9

LACE CLOAK OR MANTLE

England, 1760–1775

Black silk leno net, brocaded with self-color silk; silk ribbon; silk sewing thread; lead weights

Overall width, 52" (132.1 cm); center back length without hood, 19¼" (48.9 cm)
Neckband length, 14¾" (37.5 cm)
Selvage width, approximately 23¼" (59.1 cm)

Accession number: 1993-337

Ruffled lace cloak, overall showing hood from back.

Women sometimes wore short cloaks as light wraps and as fashionable accessories. Lace cloaks were worn in the daytime, in spite of their apparent formality.

Materials

This cloak is made of sheer black fabric yardage woven on a loom or frame to resemble lace. The ground of open leno is embellished with extra threads that form rows of alternating flowers and leaves. The sewing thread is black silk. The neckband is ribbed silk grosgrain ribbon 1⅜" wide by 14¾" long (3.5 by 37.5 cm), overlaid with layers and puffs of the lace textile for trim. Three lead weights covered with grosgrain ribbon are sewn to the hem to help the light fabric drape gracefully.

Change over Time

Despite its sheerness, the delicate textile is remarkably intact, with only a few scattered weak areas. Thread remnants around the face of the hood indicate that there was once a ruffle or other trimming sewn to the hood. The trimming may have been lace that was removed because it had become tattered. The ribbon drawstring for the neckline is missing.

Construction

Stitching: The garment is sewn with running stitches, whipstitches, and the edge finish that resembles slanted hemming stitches on the lining side and topstitching on the right side (*point à rabattre sous la main;* see p. 8).

Fashionable cloaks

Short cloaks were fashionable accessories that provided extra warmth in drafty rooms. Cloaks came in a variety of styles and materials. In Williamsburg, the most common materials advertised by local milliners were satin in white, black, blue, crimson, and spotted and flowered patterns; Persian in white and black; cloth in black, purple, scarlet, and crimson (see p. 56); and lace described as black and blond. (Blond was silk lace.) Net or lace hooded cloaks like this one are seen in eighteenth-century prints and paintings, especially those of the British artist Allan Ramsey (1713–1784). Diderot illustrates patterns for several styles of cloaks (below), including a mantelet *very similar to the one in this section. Figure 1 is the hood. Figure 2 illustrates two versions of the mantelet. Figure 3, the wider garment with arms slits, is a* pelisse.

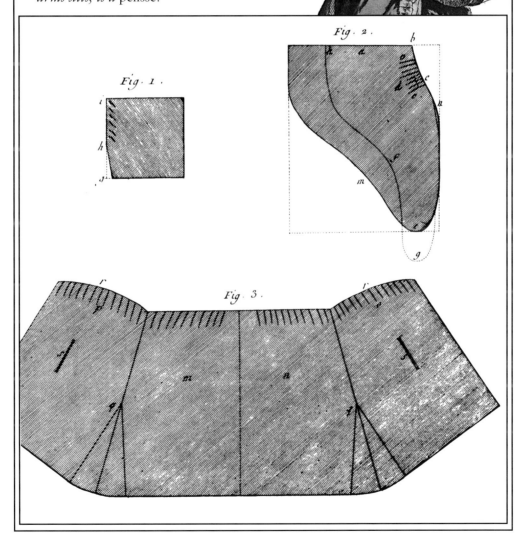

Mantle

Hood

face opening

center back   tuck between marks   center back

Ribbon

Neckband Overlay

Sketch of Trim
Applied over Neckband

Assembly Detail
(reduced scale)

Cape

center back

top edge of ruffle

weight

Ruffle Detail

154¼" (391.8 cm) long

Ruffle

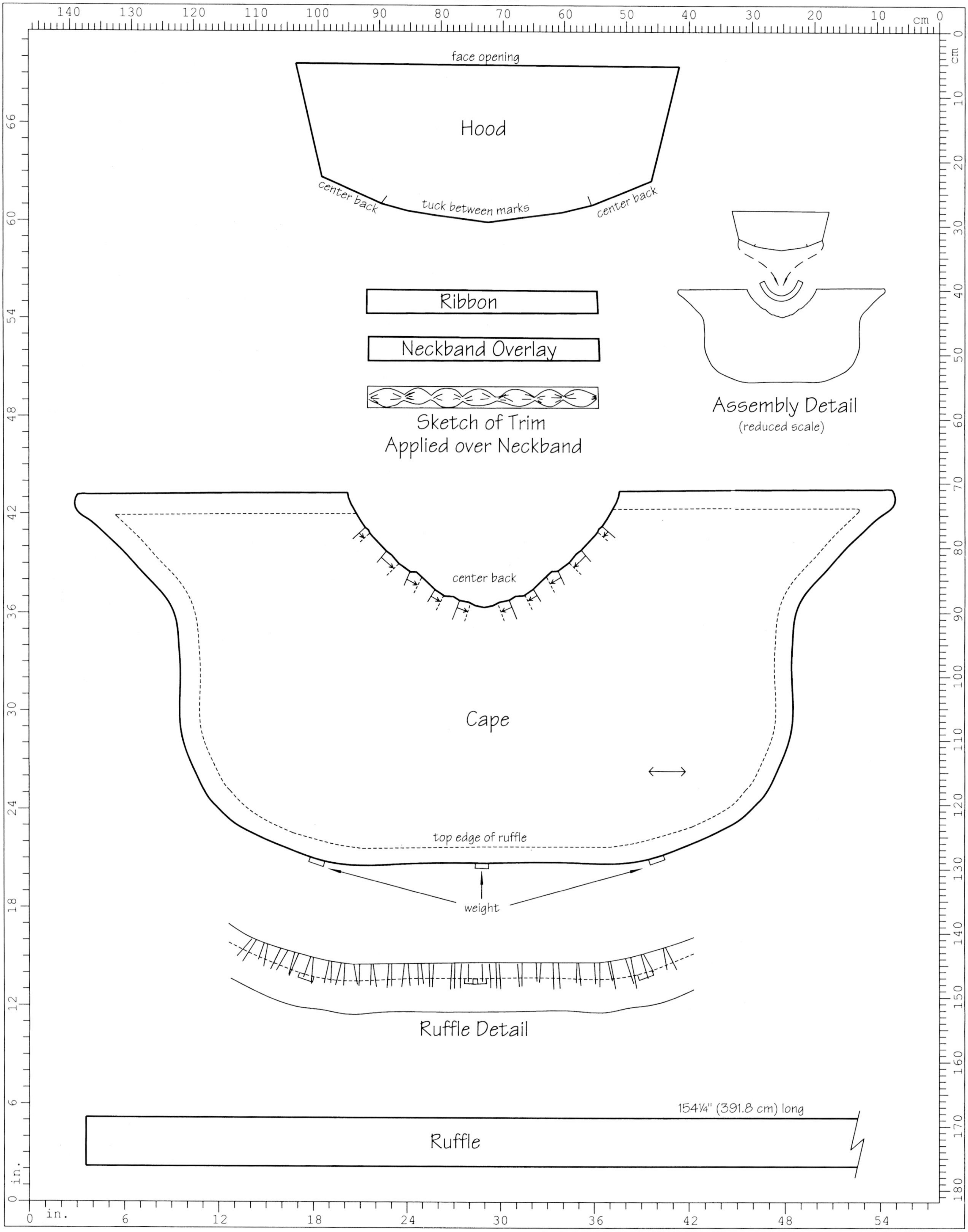

Cape: The cape or cloak body is cut in one piece and is unlined.

Trim: The cape is edged with a ruffle that measures 3" wide by 154¼" long (7.6 by 391.8 cm). The ruffle is finished with a rolled and corded hem about ¹⁄₃₂" (.8 mm) in width. The ruffle is pleated into ¼" (6 mm) tucks that are spaced at irregular intervals of 1½" to 2½" (3.8 to 6.4 cm). The upper edge of the ruffle is tacked to the cloak body at each tuck. The ruffle is attached with running stitches.

Weights: Three lead weights 1" long by ³⁄₈" wide (2.5 by 1 cm) are encased in squares of black ribbon and whipstitched to the hem of the cloak on the back side; the weights are camouflaged by the ruffle trim.

Neckband: The neckband has four layers. A black ribbed silk ribbon forms the foundation. It is hemmed at each end and overlaid on the outside with a double layer of the black lace textile, whose edges are turned under. The outside of the neckband is ornamented with puffs of gathered self-fabric trimming. The ends of the neckband are left open, forming a casing between the ribbon and the lace fabrics, intended for a ribbon drawstring around the neck.

Cape Attachment: The cape was pleated and attached to the neckband by encasing its raw edges between the ribbon and the layers of lace. It was stitched with *point à rabattre sous la main* (see p. 8).

Hood: The back seam of the hood is butted and whipstitched; the right sides were placed together and closely whipstitched over seam allowances of less than ¹⁄₃₂" (.8 mm). The hood is shaped with

Back hood and neckband. The neckband is trimmed with puffs of the lace textile.

pleats radiating from the center back seam. On the interior, the pleats are caught with stitches positioned about ¼" (6 mm) from the center of the radiating circle. The face of the hood is an unhemmed selvage edge but was once trimmed with an edging or ruffle. The hood was attached to the ribbon neckband by placing right sides together and whipstitching over a minute seam allowance.

Hem: Around the perimeters of the cape, the raw edges of the textile are pressed toward the right side and covered with the ruffle. The pressed hems measure about ¼" (6 mm). 🌢

Left: Ruffle and fabric-covered weight sewn to the back side.

❧10
CLOAK

Probably England, 1750–1810

Red broadcloth (plain-woven wool, fulled, napped, and shorn); silk sewing thread

Overall length, excluding hood, 42½" (108 cm); hem circumference, 163½" (415.3 cm)
Wool selvage width, 55" (140 cm)

Accession number: 1953-968

*Red broadcloth cloak
seen from the back.*

utilizes the full width of the textile. Cloaks of this date are not usually cut to curve over the shoulders. Arm slits in this example free the hands for work while the center front remains closed around the body for warmth. The hood is generous in size to accommodate tall hairstyles and a cap, and a casing with drawstring allows the hood to be drawn up close to the face. The back of the hood is shaped with pleats radiating from the center back in a characteristic fan.

Materials

This cloak is made of red wool broadcloth sewn with golden brown silk and fastened with replacement black ribbon ties. The silk lining was added in the twentieth century.

Change over Time

The garment has suffered from well-intentioned repairs and relining, making an exact study of the original construction problematic, although the cloak remains an excellent document for studying style and cut. It is lined with twentieth-century silk, and the arm slits have been sewn shut. Although the hems are now turned up under the new lining, the original hem was certainly left as a cut edge. Originally, the hood was lined with soft thin silk and the cloak front was faced with taffeta; there was not a full lining.

Construction

Stitching: The cloak is constructed with pale yellow silk backstitches.

Body: The cloak's body was made from a full width of 55" (140 cm) broadcloth, pieced at either side to form a large semicircle almost nine feet across. The arm slits are slashes cut into the cloth perpendicular to the seams, without any evidence of original hemming, reinforcing, or finishing. The long seams of the body were sewn with double running stitches using golden brown silk sewing thread. The neckline of the cloak body is gathered into 24" (61 cm) where it joins the hood. The gathers are concentrated at the back.

The wide, full skirts and ruffled sleeves of women's gowns made wearing an overcoat impractical if not impossible until the end of the eighteenth century, when styles became slimmer. A variety of cloaks, both short and long, answered the needs for warmth and rain protection without the difficulties of pulling a fitted garment over an elaborately trimmed gown or disarranging flounces. Like other cloaks of the eighteenth century, this one is made with a sweeping semicircular body that

Cloak

gathered into 24" (61 cm)

gathered between marks
into 11" (28 cm)

slash for arm

selvage

selvage

Cloak Body

Hood

grain direction
for small piece

Cloak Body

left side piece

Cloak Body

right side piece

Hood
Side View

face opening

pleats, center back

sewn to cloak

Cloak Assembly

(⅓ scale)

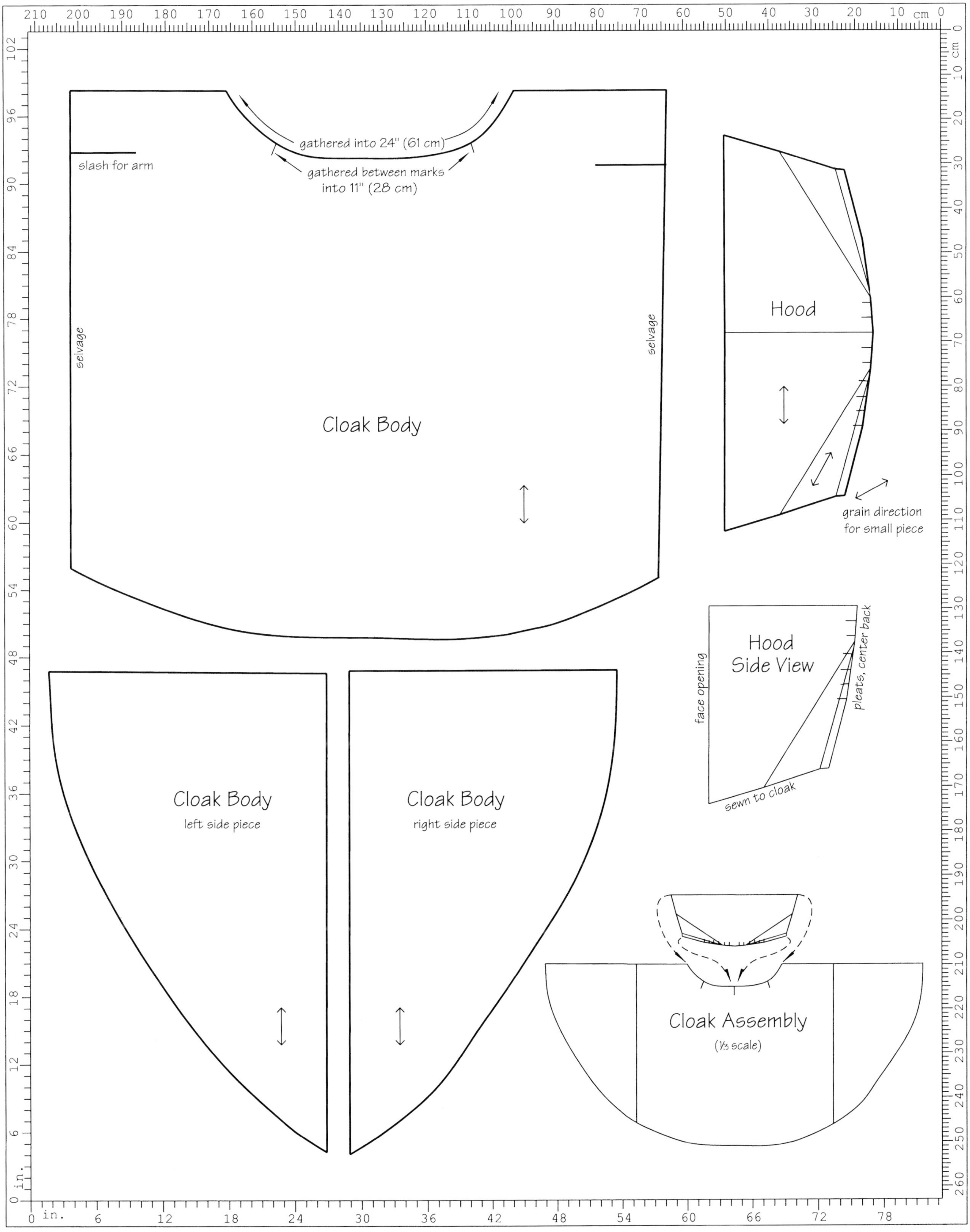

Hood: The hood is seamed up the center back, with pleats radiating at the crown. Because of the cloth's thickness, the pleats do not lie flat. The hood was pieced, probably to eke out enough fabric from the scraps left after the body pieces were cut. By piecing the hood, the entire garment was made from about 2¾ yards of 55" (140 cm) fabric.

Hem: The original hem was a cut raw edge but has now been encased in the modern lining. ☙

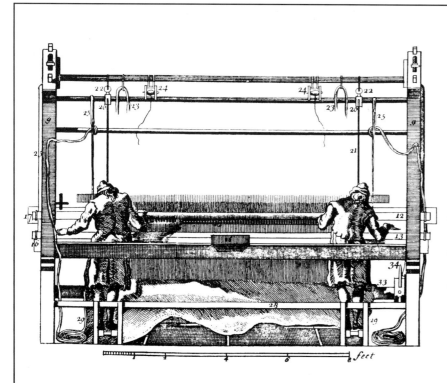

More about broadcloth

In the eighteenth century, the fabric called cloth *was a particular type of woolen textile that was woven in a plain weave, fulled (deliberately shrunk), napped to raise a fuzzy texture, shorn close to the surface, and pressed. The resulting textile was dense, warm, and water-repellent, with a smooth, feltlike appearance. Cloth was considered appropriate for men's fine suits, cloaks, and writing surfaces on furniture, the latter often dyed green. Because the fulling process matted the fibers together, good-quality cloth did not ravel when cut, so hems and seams did not require any further finishing. Although cloth resembles felt, the two fabrics differ substantially. Cloth is first woven on a loom, and felt is not woven. Eighteenth-century cloth was often woven on wide two-man looms, hence the name* broadcloth. *England was famous for the production of fine woolen cloth textiles that were exported around the world, including to the American colonies.*

11

SHIFT

England or America, 1780–1810

White plain-woven linen; linen sewing thread

Overall length, 47" (119.4 cm); width, 44" (111.8 cm); skirt hem circumference, 79¼" (201.3 cm)
Linen selvage width, 30½" (77.5 cm)

Accession number: 1986-207

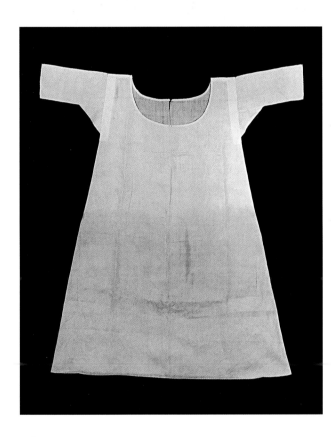

Change over Time

The garment is very thin and fragile, betraying its many years of being washed, ironed, and folded for storage. Old folds caused long tears in the brittle linen, requiring conservation treatment. The fact that the shift has not been altered makes it an excellent study document. The neckline drawstring is missing.

Left: *Linen shift seen from the front.*

Construction

Stitching: The sleeve and side seams are sewn with 16 to 20 running stitches per inch (2.5 cm). All seams are exceptionally small with the raw edges turned inside and felled. The completed seams measure about ¹⁄₁₆" (1.6 mm) wide. Other stitches include butting and whipstitching, backstitching, and slanted hemming.

Cut: The shift was shaped to flare at the hems by taking the triangles that were left over from cutting the upper body and adding them as gores to the lower portions of the skirt. Square gussets folded on the bias are stitched under the arms to allow ease of movement.

A shift made of white linen or cotton was the bottom layer of a woman's multilayered ensemble, acting as a washable liner to protect the outer clothing from perspiration and body soil. With all the layers in place, the gown or petticoat never actually touched the skin. Equally important, the shift protected the wearer's skin from abrasion by the boned stays, hoops, woolen petticoats, and other discomforts of fashionable clothing. Many women slept in the same shifts they wore during the day, whereas those with larger wardrobes had separate nightshifts. Shifts were considered underwear. They were not worn exposed in public except by slave women working in rural areas and free women far removed from public settings.

Materials

The shift is made of fine white linen with a thread count of 88 warps by 88 wefts per inch (2.5 cm) and a selvage width of 30½" (77.5 cm). The shift is sewn with linen.

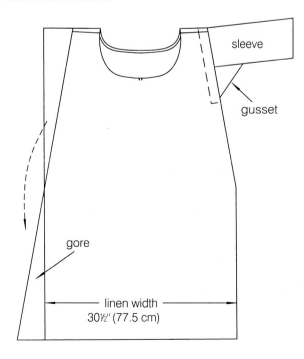

Shifts were assembled to make economical use of the textile.

The drawing at right and the photograph below show the neckline bound with linen tape to accomodate a drawstring. Reinforcements are sewn on the outside top shoulder. Additional reinforcements are sewn on the inside butting the sleeve (seen at the far right in the photograph below).

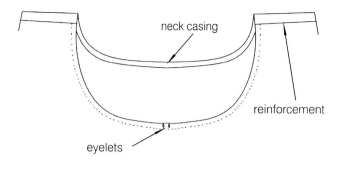

neck casing

reinforcement

eyelets

Neckline: The neckline has a casing made of straight-grain linen tape ⁵⁄₁₆" (8 mm) wide, sewn to the wrong side and seamed at the center front. This casing accommodates a drawstring (missing in this example). Two elongated eyelets located at center front on the outside of the neckline allow the drawstring to be adjusted from the front.

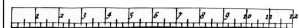

About linen width

After shrinkage has been taken into account, the width of the linen in this shift corresponds roughly to the period designation of 7/8 linen, which means that the linen is ⁷⁄₈ yard wide. Calculated another way, it is 7 times 4½" (⅛ yard), for a total of 31½". Other standard linen widths were yard wide (36"), 3/4 (3 times ¼ yard, or 27"), and 5/4 (5 times ¼ yard, or 45"). Manufacturers did not always conform to exact standards, however, and consumers occasionally complained that textiles were not quite as wide as their designations.

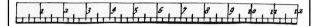

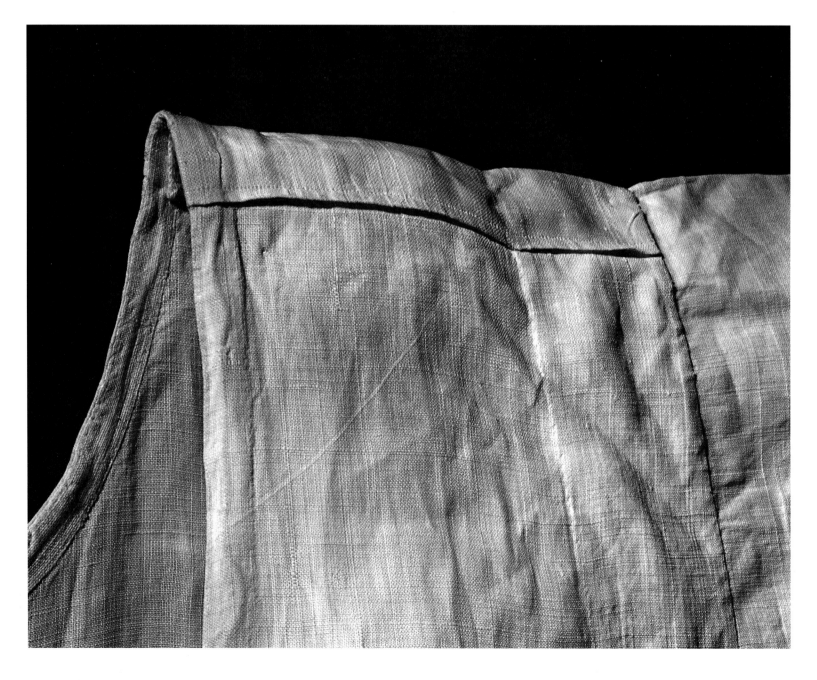

Shift

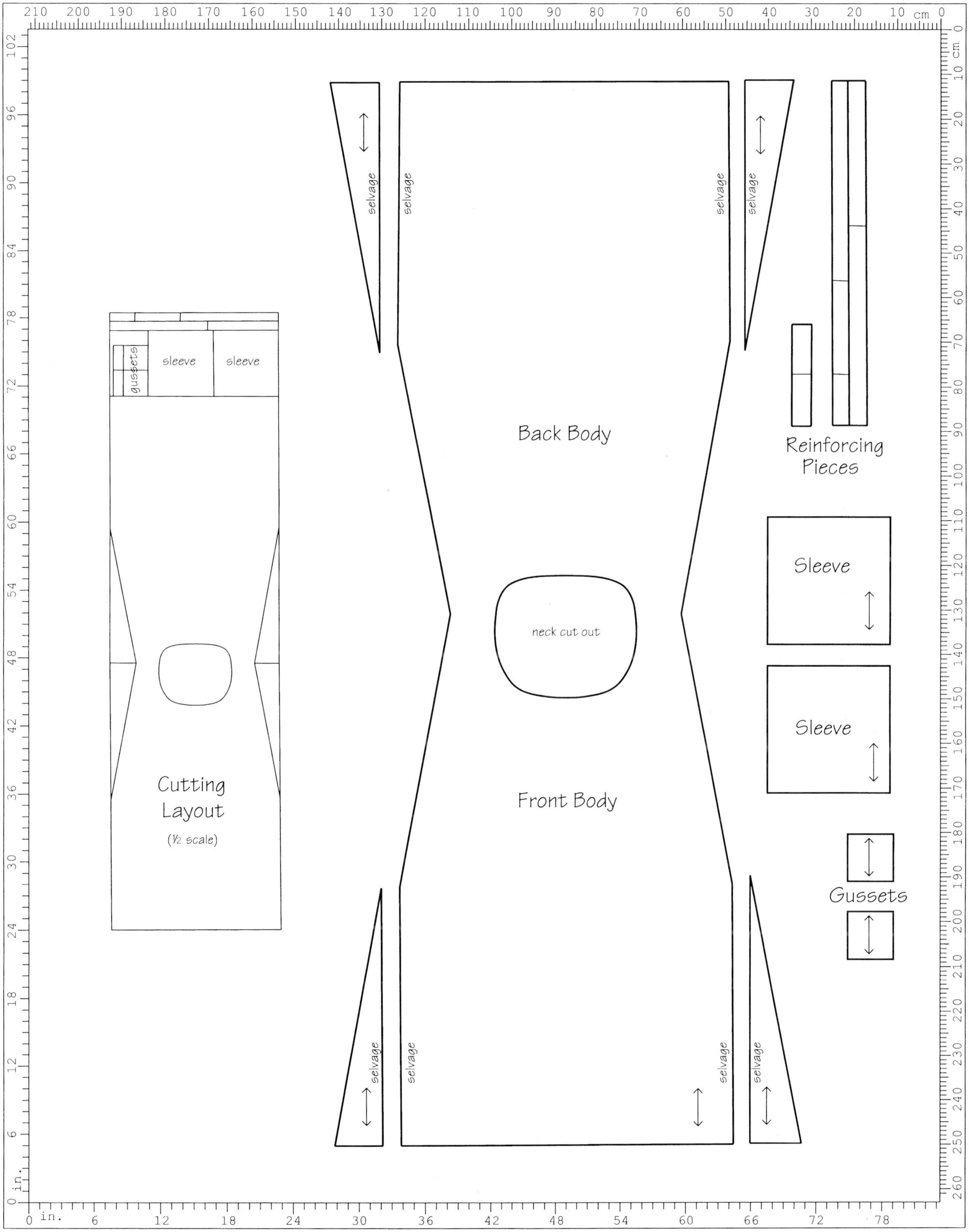

Back Body
Front Body
neck cut out
selvage
selvage
selvage
selvage
selvage
selvage
selvage
selvage
Reinforcing Pieces
Sleeve
Sleeve
Gussets
Cutting Layout
(½ scale)
sleeve
sleeve
gussets
cm
in.

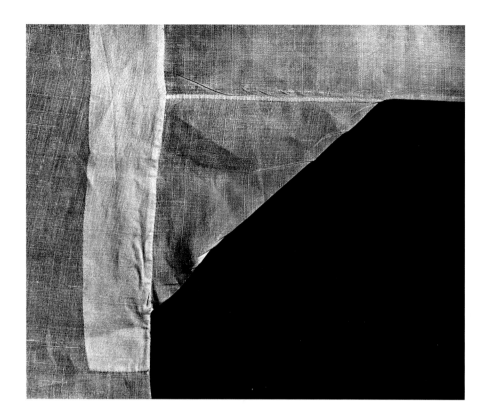

Gusset under the proper left sleeve. The vertical linen reinforcement sewn on the inside is seen as a shadow through the thin linen.

Reinforcements: Reinforcing pieces 4" by 1⅛" (10.2 by 2.9 cm) are sewn on the outside shoulder from neckline to sleeve and are topstitched with backstitches. Additional reinforcement strips 21½" by 1½" (54.6 by 3.8 cm) are sewn on the inside where the sleeves and gusset join the body. The sleeve gusset reinforcements have their raw edges turned under and stitched to the shift body with slanted hemming stitches. The reinforcements were pieced to conserve the fabric.

Gores: The gores of the skirt were constructed with the selvages butted and whipstitched.

Hems: The hems of the sleeves and skirt were turned under twice and sewn with slanted hemming stitches. The hems measure about ¹⁄₁₆" (1.6 mm) wide. 🖋

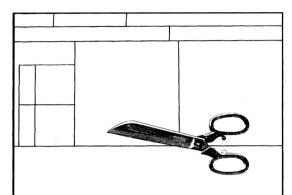

Cutting and sewing personal linens

Although plain in appearance, shifts are fascinating studies in period cutting and sewing techniques. Fabric cost a great deal in comparison to labor, and shifts were carefully cut to avoid wasting more than a few inches of the expensive fabric. Shifts were made of rectangles, squares, and triangles that fit on the linen like a crossword puzzle. Eighteenth-century records reveal that adult women's shifts nearly always required from 3¼ to 3½ yards (297 to 320 cm) of

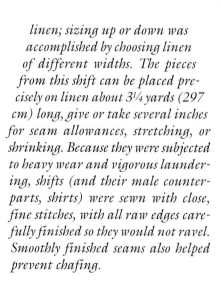

linen; sizing up or down was accomplished by choosing linen of different widths. The pieces from this shift can be placed precisely on linen about 3¼ yards (297 cm) long, give or take several inches for seam allowances, stretching, or shrinking. Because they were subjected to heavy wear and vigorous laundering, shifts (and their male counterparts, shirts) were sewn with close, fine stitches, with all raw edges carefully finished so they would not ravel. Smoothly finished seams also helped prevent chafing.

$\stackrel{\text{♊}}{\text{12}}$
STAYS

England, 1740–1760

Lavender wool satin; linen; boning (probably baleen); linen sewing thread; silk sewing thread; leather

Center front length, 13½" (34.3 cm); chest, 33"–34" (83.8–86.4 cm)
Waist, 28¼"–29½" (71.8–73.7 cm)

Accession number: 1966-188

Left: *Boned stays shown flat. The eyelets meet at the center back.*

The stays are posi-tioned for spiral lacing, probably starting from the bottom with a half-hitch knot in the lower left eyelet and ending at the upper right.

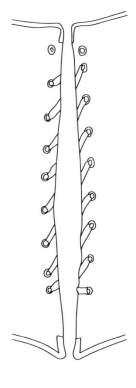

These stays are characteristic of those used in the third quarter of the eighteenth century. They do not have cups for the bust but instead create the desirable figure of a smooth, inverted cone. Although most stays laced up the back in the spiral pattern seen here, some laced up the front for ease and convenience. Because of the strength required to push baleen into the stitched channels, stays were usually made by professional male stay makers. Surprisingly, stays were not necessarily made to order for the individual; many were sold as ready-made items and were often exported to the colonies from England.

Materials

The stays are made with an outer layer of lavender worsted satin, pressed to a high shine. There are two inner layers of linen, and a third layer of linen forms the lining. The boning is probably baleen. The channels are stitched with natural-color silk; other sewing thread is natural-color linen. White leather covers the seams and binds the edges; some tabs retain their original leather lining on the back.

Change over Time

The original lavender color has faded to pink. Insect damage has opened small holes in the wool, revealing some of the linen inner layers. Some seams are covered by leather strips, and others are covered with ½" (6 mm) wide linen tape. The linen tapes probably are replacements. The linen lining is stained from wear but is probably an early replacement. Sections of the linen lining are repaired with twentieth-century thread.

Construction

Stitching: The stays are sewn with backstitches, slip stitches, running stitches, and overcast eyelet stitches.

Eyelets: The eyelets are worked with heavy linen thread that has been overcast around punched holes. (They are not worked with buttonhole stitching.) The eyelets are laced through with protective leather strips that prevent excessive abrasion and stress from lacing and wear. There are nine eyelets on each side, spaced so that only the top and bottom pairs are across from each other; the remaining are offset for spiral lacing.

1966-188

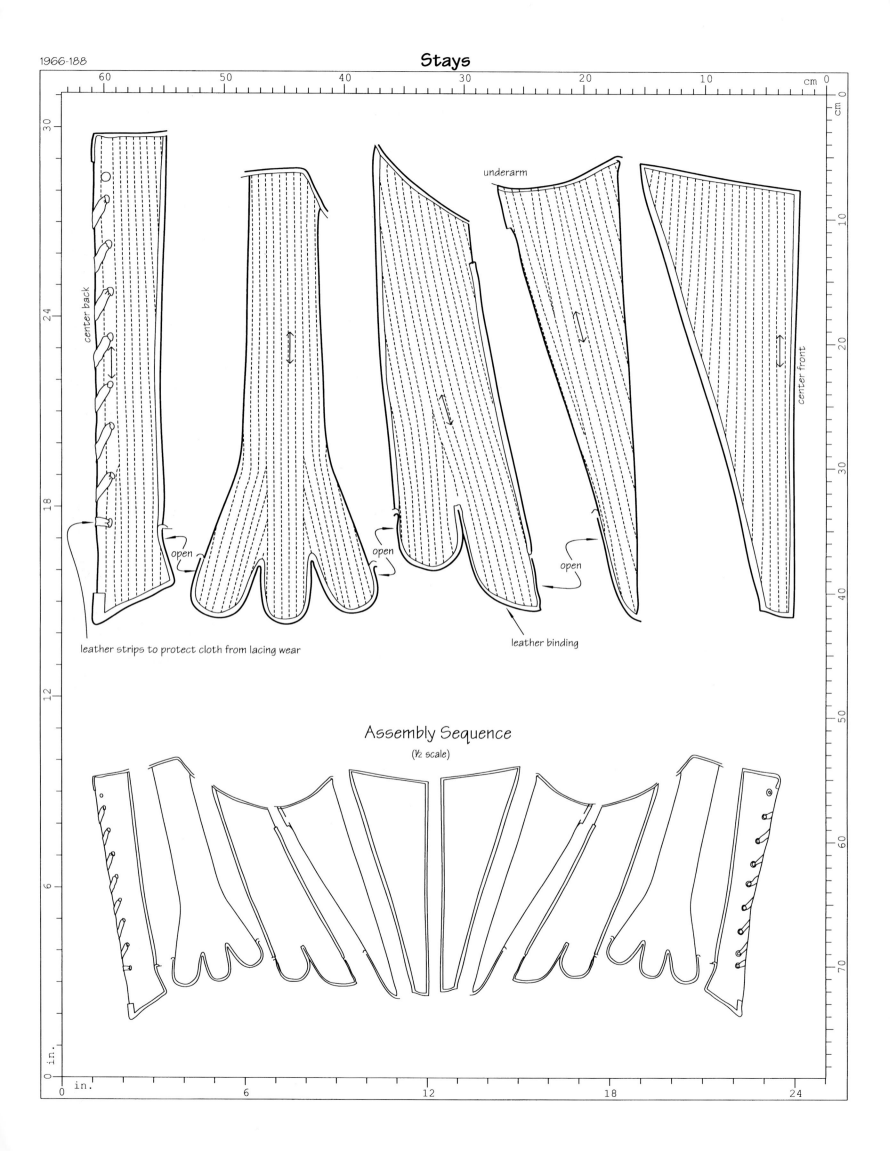

center back

underarm

open
open
open

leather strips to protect cloth from lacing wear

leather binding

center front

Assembly Sequence

(½ scale)

Panels: The stays are made as a series of layered panels. Each panel was constructed individually before being joined to the others. The stays are very heavy and consist of five layers altogether. From outside to inside the layers are lavender worsted satin, plain-woven linen, boning (probably baleen), sized linen, and a loose linen lining. The first four layers are stitched together by 10 silk backstitches per inch (2.5 cm), arranged in rows or channels. The boned panels are butted together and sewn. These butted joining seams are covered with leather strips or linen plain-woven tape, stitched down with running stitches.

Lining: The loose lining (worn next to the skin) was folded under and attached at the edges with slip stitches and could easily be replaced if soiled. The lining is pieced at the side seams and tabs. Leather lines the tabs that splay out over the hips.

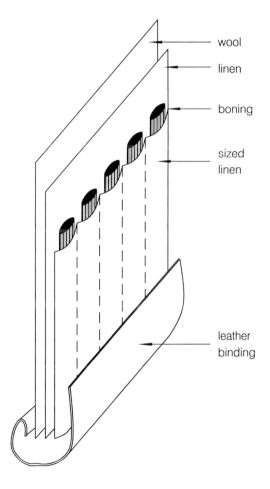

wool

linen

boning

sized linen

leather binding

Binding: The outside edges are bound with leather, probably to keep the baleen from cutting through the fabric and irritating the skin. The leather binding was stitched with right sides together, folded over the raw edges to the back, and sewn with slanted hemming stitches. The cut edges of leather are covered by the lining. ☙

Lower back of stays showing the eyelets, leather binding on the edges, and a strip overlaying the seam.

Left: *A leather strip binds all but the removable lining of the stays. The lining is not shown in the drawing.*

63

About tight lacing

Much has been said about tight lacing and tiny waists in the eighteenth century. Prints like this one satirized and exaggerated the fashion. Most women, however, had to move about, work, and care for children on a daily basis and therefore did not follow the practice of tight lacing. Of all the stays in the Colonial Williamsburg collection, the smallest waist size is 24" (61 cm), and one pair has a waist of 35" (76.2 cm). Although stays certainly could be sized and laced to constrict the waist and thus impede movement, only the very fashionable carried tight lacing to extremes. In fact, eighteenth-century stays did not bind the waist as much as corsets in the Victorian period of the nineteenth century. With her stays, the woman in the print wears a thin linen shift, fringed under petticoat, and a large pocket stuffed with personal items.

Fashious

Victim a Satire

TIGHT LACING, or FASHION before EASE.
From the Original Picture by John Collet, in the possession of the Proprietors.

362   Printed for & Sold by Bowles & Carver, at their Map & Print Warehouse, N.º 69 in S.t Pauls Church Yard. London. —   Published as the Act direct.

Detail, quilted petticoat no. 5.

Bodice back, gown no. 3.

Gown no. 3 and petticoat no. 4.

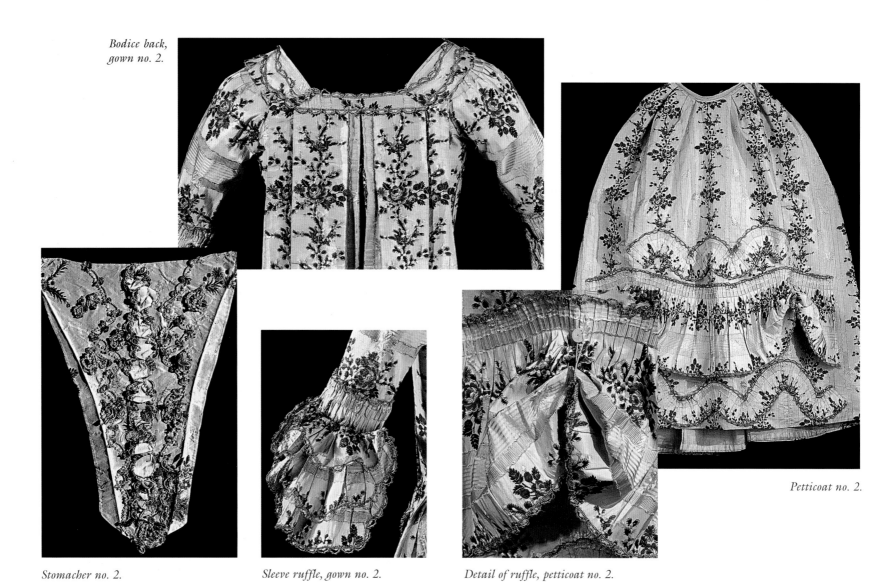

Bodice back,
gown no. 2.

Petticoat no. 2.

Stomacher no. 2.

Sleeve ruffle, gown no. 2.

Detail of ruffle, petticoat no. 2.

Cloak no. 10, shown full width.

Jacket no. 6.

Detail of shoulder, jacket no. 6.

Short gown no. 7.

Apron no. 8.

Detail of embroidery, pocket no. 13.

Detail of lacing eyelets, stays no. 12.

Right and wrong sides of clocks, stockings no. 16.

ꙮ13
Pocket

New England, 1740–1770

White plain-woven linen-and-cotton; crewel wool; plain-woven linen backing and interlining; printed and striped cotton bindings; linen sewing thread

Length, 17½" (44.4 cm); width, 14" (35.6 cm)

Accession number: 1963-11

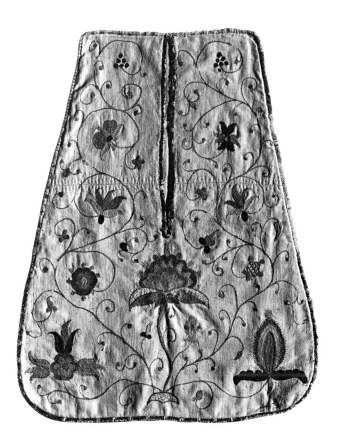

Eighteenth-century pockets were generous bags that women and girls tied around their waists beneath their petticoats. The wearer reached her pockets through openings or slits in her skirts. Pockets were not sewn into skirts until the nineteenth century, possibly because pockets stuffed with paraphernalia would have distorted the fashionable wide skirts of the eighteenth century and ruined their line. Pockets varied in size and decoration, ranging from plain, sturdy cotton *dimity* to more decorative printed textiles and embroidery. They were often worn in pairs.

Materials

The face of the pocket is made from a natural-color textile plain-woven with a linen warp and a cotton weft. It is embroidered with colored crewel wool. The pocket is lined and interlined with plain-woven linens and bound with narrow strips of patterned cotton, pieced together.

Change over Time

This pocket shows wear at the binding edges, especially in the dark colors, where iron mordant has weakened the textiles. No ties survive. It is not known whether the pocket was originally one of a pair. The woolen needlework has shrunk in places from washing, distorting the ground fabric.

Left: Woman's pocket embroidered with crewel wool.

About pockets and children

Pockets were separate pieces tied under the skirt but not attached to it. This practice explains how Lucy Locket lost her pocket in the traditional nursery rhyme below.

Little girls also wore pockets. On a hot July day in 1774, a tutor observed one of his young students: "The wind itself seems to be heated! . . . I laugh'd cordially to see the contrivance of Fanny, the loveliest of them all, to grow cool, She sat on a low bench, & put her Hand in her pocket, & seem'd exceeding diligent in looking for something—But before She took out her hand She had off both her Stockings, & left them both in her pocket!"

Lucy Locket lost her pocket;
Kitty Fisher found it.
Not a penny was there in it,
Only ribbon round it.

open and stitched down with running stitches. The back of the pocket is plain-woven linen, pieced together from three fragments using felled seams.

Interlining and Back: Inside the pocket, the decorative embroidered face was interlined with linen to strengthen it and perhaps to prevent the pocket's contents from snagging and abrading the back of the needlework. The decorated front and interlining were treated as one for construction. They were slashed through both layers and bound for the pocket opening. The back piece of linen is joined to the front with edge binding.

Binding: The pocket's opening and outside edges are bound with various striped and printed cottons, cut on the straight grain and pieced together to gain sufficient length to go all the way around the pocket and slash, approximately 74" (188 cm). The bindings vary in width from ³⁄₈" to ¹⁄₂" (1 to 1.3 cm), excluding an unknown amount turned inside for seam allowances. The bindings were stitched to the pocket with running stitches and with the right sides of the bindings against the right side of the pocket. The bindings were turned to the back to encase all the layers and sewn to the back of the pocket with slanted hemming stitches. The bindings are not topstitched. 🐝

Pocket detail. Both the front and back are pieced. The edges and slit are bound with printed cotton.

Construction

Stitching: The pocket is constructed with running stitches, backstitches, and slip stitches.

Embroidery: The pocket front is embroidered with crewel wool using outline; seed; buttonhole; and flat, or self-couching (also known as *Roumanian* and *New England laid*), stitches. The thin tendrils and the outside edges of most of the flowers and leaves are worked with outline stitch. Larger motifs are filled in solidly with satin stitches, shaded from light to dark. Small berries are not outlined but are worked with flat stitches. Some flowers are outlined with buttonhole stitches that are widely spaced and turned so that the legs form a thorny edge around the motif.

Piecing: The pocket is constructed of pieced-together scraps of linen and cotton. The ground fabric is pieced under the embroidery, indicating that the pocket top was first assembled, then embroidered. The piecing seam was sewn with backstitches, then the seam allowances were pressed

Right: *The pocket layers are held together with staight-grain binding sewn to the outer edges.*

front, interlining, and back layers

binding

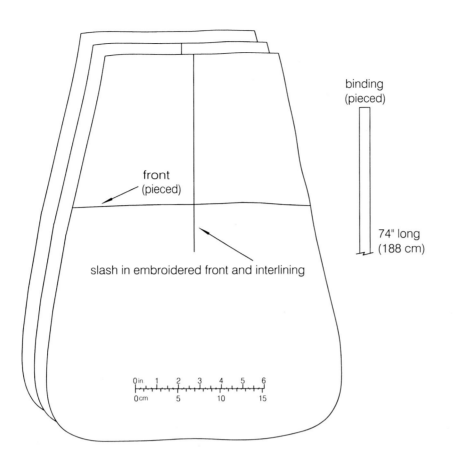

binding
(pieced)

74" long
(188 cm)

front
(pieced)

slash in embroidered front and interlining

| 0 in | 1 | 2 | 3 | 4 | 5 | 6 |

| 0 cm | 5 | 10 | 15 |

The pocket consists of three pattern pieces of identical outline—an embroidered front, an interlining, and a backing. The narrow cotton binding joins all of the pieces at the outside edges.

Getting dressed

Dress clothing comprised multiple pieces that were layered to create a fashionable posture and silhouette. Women's and girls' outfits often included a shift, stockings, shoes, stays, one or two pockets, hoops or an underpetticoat, a gown petticoat intended to be visible, gown, stomacher, cap, mitts, and apron. The drawings show typical clothing of a well-to-do girl around the middle of the eighteenth century.

1963-11

Embroidery Pattern and Binding Scheme

printed binding, pieced

cm 0
40   30   20   10   cm
18
12
6
in.
0 in.
0   6   12
10
20
30
40
50

🌱14
HOOP PETTICOAT

New York, 1755–1785

Descended in Van Rensselaer family of Albany and vicinity; possibly worn by Anne Van Rensselaer (1766–1855)

Natural-color plain-woven linen; split cane; linen twill tape; woolen batting; linen sewing thread

Center front length, 33½" (85 cm); waist adjustable from 22 to 35" (55.9 to 88.9 cm)
Top hoop casing, 49½" (125.7 cm); middle hoop casing, 66" (167.6 cm); bottom hoop casing, 77" (195.6 cm)
Linen selvage width, 31½" (80 cm)

Accession number: 1990-11

During much of the eighteenth century, fashionable women's gowns had full skirts with the fullness concentrated at the side hips. The skirts required support to achieve this silhouette, and hoop petticoats were one way to produce the desired shape. The typical hoop petticoat was a linen skirt with channels sewn into it and oval bands of cane or other material suspended in the channels. This petticoat originally had four hoops of graduated sizes. It dips slightly at the front waist and ties at the center back. If the wearer chose to put pockets under the petticoat, she could reach them though padded openings at the sides.

A typed tag sewn to the inside yoke of the hoops reads, "Property of Mrs. Annie Vanrensselaer Wells Ossining-on-Hudson New York." These hoops have a tradition of being owned by Anne Van Cortlandt Van Rensselaer (1766–1855) of New York State. She may have received them from an older relative. Her husband, Philip, was later the mayor of Albany. The hoops were handed down in the family through the original owner's sister to the latter's granddaughter, Mrs. Alexander (Annie) Wells. Annie Wells wrote the note and sewed it into the hoops sometime after her marriage in 1864.

Materials

The petticoat is constructed of plain-woven linen with a waist drawstring made from ½" (1.3 cm) wide linen plain-woven tape. The cane hoops were split lengthwise and bent in an open oval shape; they are covered by linen casings. Padded pocket slits at the hips are stuffed with wool batting. The hoops are sewn with linen thread.

Change over Time

The linen is slightly discolored. The second hoop is broken at the center front. The two lower hoops are missing entirely, leaving empty linen casings. Although some of the stitches fastening the hoop casings to the petticoat are missing, the position of missing hoops can be inferred from old stitch holes and creases in the skirt. Such construction folds and wrinkles are important evidence to preserve.

Hoop petticoat, front view, photographed on black mount.

Construction

Stitching: The hoops are constructed with running stitches, whipstitches, and slanted hemming stitches using linen thread.

Yoke: The skirt falls from a shaped yoke made of four separate pieces. The yoke fastens around the waist with linen tape that ties at the center back. The waist casing was created by folding down the top ¾" (1.9 cm) of the yoke, turning under the

Hoop Petticoat

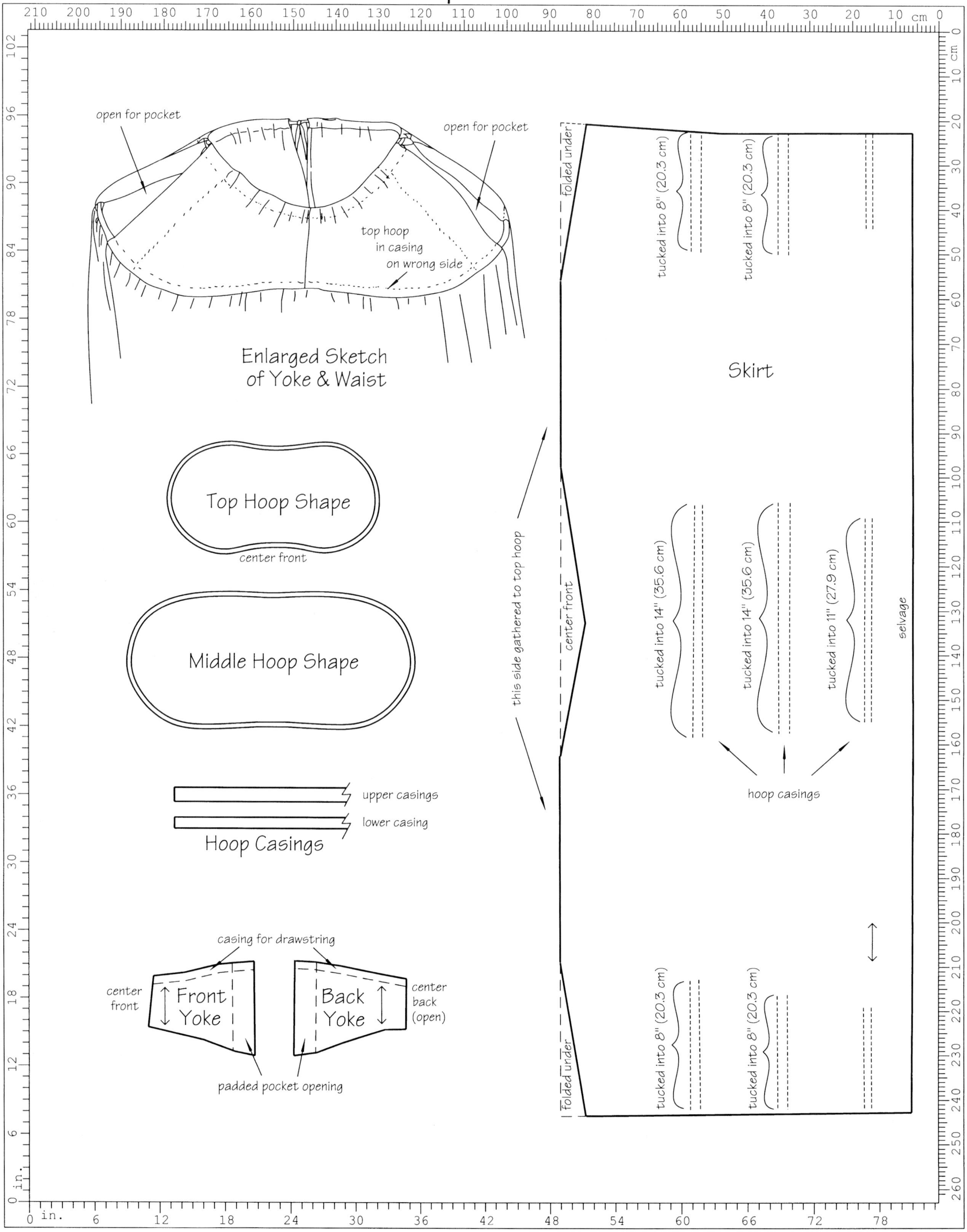

open for pocket

open for pocket

top hoop
in casing
on wrong side

Enlarged Sketch
of Yoke & Waist

Top Hoop Shape

center front

Middle Hoop Shape

upper casings

lower casing

Hoop Casings

casing for drawstring

center
front

Front
Yoke

Back
Yoke

center
back
(open)

padded pocket opening

folded under

tucked into 8" (20.3 cm)

tucked into 8" (20.3 cm)

Skirt

this side gathered to top hoop

center front

tucked into 14" (35.6 cm)

tucked into 14" (35.6 cm)

tucked into 11" (27.9 cm)

selvage

hoop casings

Folded under

tucked into 8" (20.3 cm)

tucked into 8" (20.3 cm)

raw edges, and stitching with slanted hemming stitches. The front seam of the yoke is sewn with closely spaced running stitches. The seam allowance varies in width from ⅝" to 1¼" (1.6 to 3.2 cm) and is pressed open. The edges (selvages) are sewn down with slanted hemming stitches. The side pocket openings have 2" (5 cm) hems that form casings for woolen batting.

Skirt: The lower skirt of the petticoat is a length of linen 31½" wide by 86¾" long (80 by 220.3 cm). The lengthwise grain runs around the body, and the skirt is gathered into 49½" (125.7z cm). The gathered skirt is butted and whipstitched to the yoke and the top hoop casing.

Hoops: The top hoop and its linen casing are stitched at the seam where the yoke and skirt meet. There were originally four hoops, but the bottom two are missing. Only their casings remain to indicate their size and position. The three lower hoops were similarly shaped and encased in linen but were stitched to the petticoat skirt only at the front and back, thus remaining free to move at the sides; the skirt was tucked slightly where the casings were stitched. The top three hoops were made of double cane encased in linen that was stitched lengthwise down the center to create twin channels for the paired canes. Evidence from the surviving linen channel indicates that the bottom hoop had a single cane; the channel is not stitched lengthwise to accommodate a double hoop.

Closure: The back of the petticoat is open from the waist to the hem. The raw edges are turned under ⅛" (3 mm) and stitched with slanted hemming stitches. When the petticoat was worn, the projecting end of each hoop was inserted into the corresponding open casing, creating an unbroken oval.

Hem: The selvage forms the bottom finish. 🌰

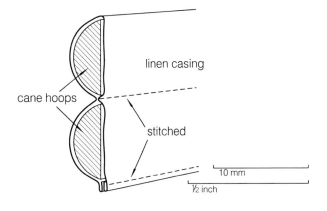

Back closure showing projecting hoops that slide into the adjacent casings to align the halves.

Left: Interior showing waist casing, padded pocket slit, and fabric-covered hoop stitched to the skirt.

Lower right: Cross section of cane hoop and linen casing.

71

❦15

Mitts

England, 1760–1780

White and blue ribbed silk; white leather lining; blue silk embroidery thread; silk sewing thread

Length, 13¾" (35 cm); width, 4¾" (12 cm)

Accession number: 1985-216, 1-2

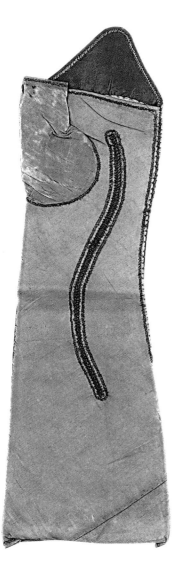

Change over Time

Mitts are subjected to great stress during wear, since they are stretched and tugged over the hands. These mitts are in very fragile condition. The silk is abraded and breaking, particularly on the thumb. Fragile areas have been supported with sheer silk.

Construction

Stitching: The mitts were constructed with running stitches, fagoting, herringbone stitches, and slanted hemming stitches. The fagoting and herringbone stitches were both decorative and functional, serving to hold the seamed pieces together.

Cut: The mitts were cut on the bias for elasticity. The silk was pieced together with running stitches, probably to utilize fully a narrow silk textile.

Lining: Except for the points, the mitts are lined with thin, white leather, cut about ⅛" (3 mm) smaller all around. The seams of the leather lining were worked with widely spaced whipstitches, leaving seam allowances of less than ⅛" (3 mm), and butting in some areas.

Silk mitts shown front and back.

Mitts were not only protective arm coverings, they were also fashionable women's accessories. By leaving the fingers and the tip of the thumb uncovered, mitts provided warmth without affecting dexterity for fine tasks such as needlework. Mitts were often worn with the points turned back over the hands.

Materials

The mitts are made of cream-color ribbed silk embroidered with blue silk. The points are faced with blue ribbed silk. Except for the points, the mitts are fully lined with thin, white leather.

Right: *Right mitt showing embroidery on back of hand, thumb and side seams, and point turned back.*

72

1985-216

40   30   20   10   cm   0

18

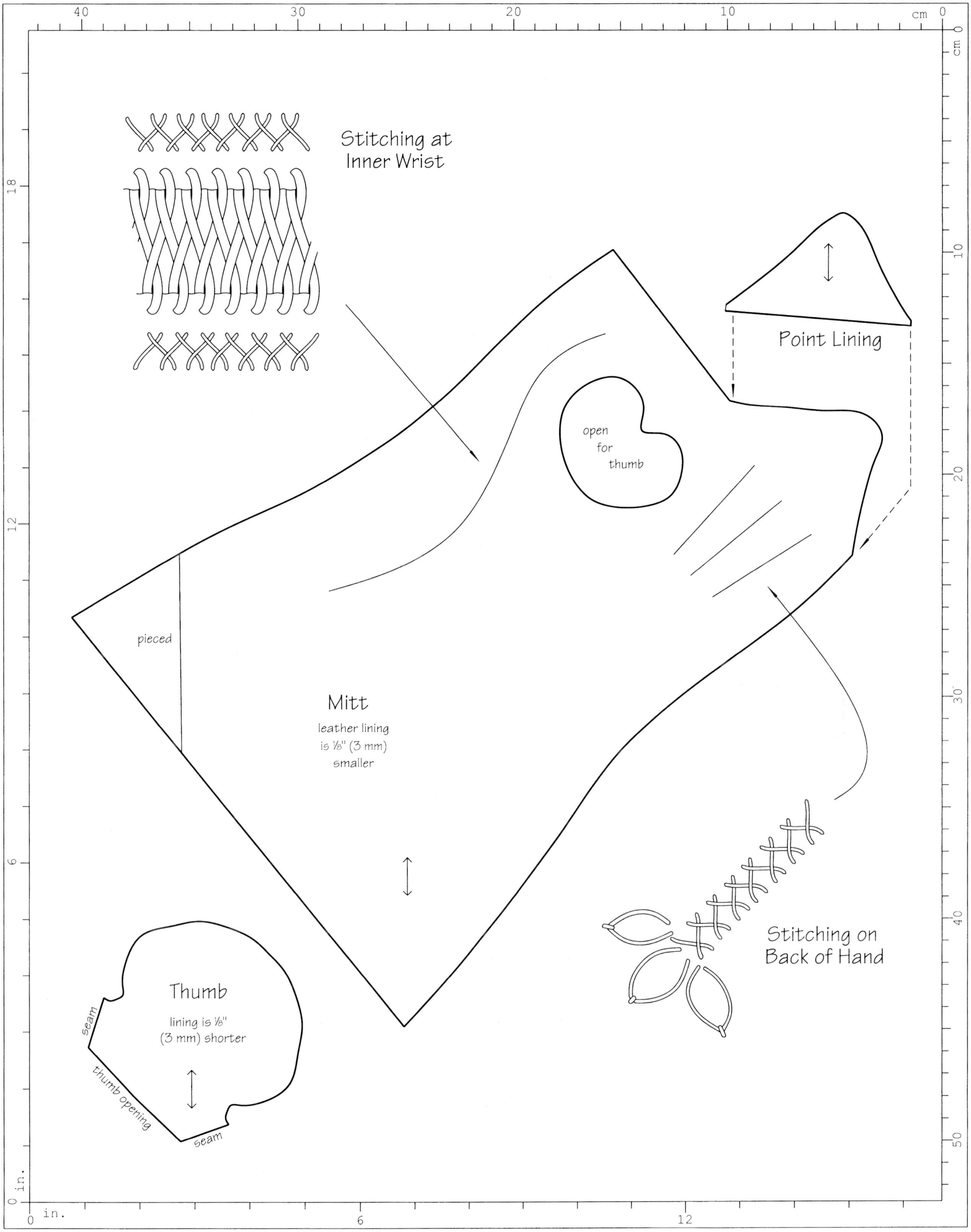

Stitching at
Inner Wrist

Point Lining

open
for
thumb

pieced

Mitt

leather lining
is ⅛" (3 mm)
smaller

Thumb

lining is ⅛"
(3 mm) shorter

seam

thumb opening

seam

Stitching on
Back of Hand

in.

0   6   12

Hems and Seams: All of the hems in the silk were turned under and sewn in decorative herringbone stitches using blue silk thread. The herringbone stitches are about ⅛" (3 mm) from the edge. On the inside wrist, a curved slit was cut into the silk. Its raw edges were turned under and hemmed with herringbone stitches, creating an opening about ¼" (6 mm) wide that was rejoined with fagoting for elasticity. The leather lining extends behind the slash to support and back the opening. The lengthwise seam running up the side of the arm was worked with fagoting that joined all the layers and gave some stretch for pulling on the mitts. Decorative stitching on the top of the hand was worked through the silk but not the leather lining.

Thumb: The thumb was lined, seamed, and basted in with long running stitches using cream silk. After basting, herringbone stitches were worked through all silk layers to hold the thumb firmly in place.

Assembly: Close study of the mitts indicates the order in which they were made. The silk outsides and the leather linings were cut as flat pieces. The thumbs were set into each piece separately. The points of the cream silk were lined with blue silk and all of the blue decorative stitching, except for the fagoted side seams, was done. After the decorative stitching was completed, the leather linings were applied. Each lining was laid in, slipped inside the thumb, and then sewn in place around all of the open edges using slanted hemming stitches. The last step was to fasten the long seam on the outside of the arm with fagoting. 🪡

Right-hand mitt with thumb turned down to show seaming. The curved line of fagoting provides elasticity.

Mitts for ladies and children

A milliner in Williamsburg, Virginia, advertised in 1768 that she had just imported from London "coloured, white silk, French kid, lamb gloves and mits for Ladies, girls, and children." Besides the pair described in this section, Colonial Williamsburg has eighteenth-century women's mitts made of black silk, yellow silk, knitted linen, and knitted silk. The collection also contains tiny mitts for children. The children's mitts, some undoubtedly made as part of christening sets, are made of linen, cotton, silk with silk embroidery, and bobbin lace. Several pairs of nineteenth-century mitts are of netted or knitted silk.

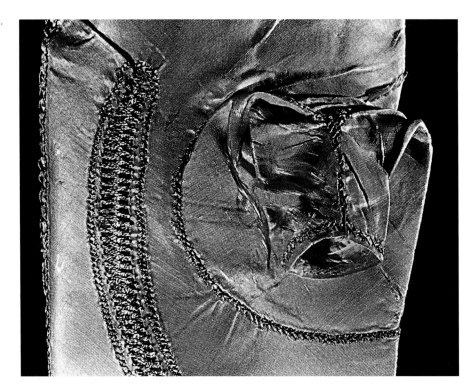

❧16
WOMEN'S OR MEN'S STOCKINGS

England, ca. 1750

Coral frame-knitted silk; blue silk clocks; silk sewing thread

Overall length with foot extended, 25" (63.5 cm); foot length, 8½"–9" (21.6–22.9 cm)

Accession number: 1975-182

Stockings were highly visible accessories, especially for eighteenth-century men, whose lower legs were revealed by knee-length breeches. Women's stockings also showed when the sway of a hoop petticoat permitted others a peek at the wearer's ankles. The finest stockings were knitted of silk and decorated at the ankles with *clocks*, decorative embroidery or knitted-in designs. Stockings were available in many materials and qualities. They were knitted in linen (also called *thread*), wool, silk, or cotton. Stockings could be purchased ready-made from milliners in a variety of styles. Catherine Rathell, a Williamsburg milliner, got her supply of stockings directly from London. In 1772 she ordered "2 Dozn. of White Ribed Silk Hose, half with, & half without Floward Clocks at 12/6." They could be hand-knitted with needles or made on a stocking frame. Less expensive stockings were also made of woven textiles such as linen or wool, cut on the bias, and sewn with seams up the back and around the foot.

Materials

These stockings are made of frame-knitted silk and are seamed with silk.

Change over Time

The stockings are somewhat faded and stained and have a few mended holes. Some of the mends appear to date from the eighteenth century.

Construction

Knitting: The stockings were knitted in stockinette stitch. There are 246 stitches around the top of the stocking, or about 27 stitches per inch (2.5 cm).

Production and Seaming: These stockings were knitted on a stocking frame as flat, shaped pieces. The curved edges were joined to form the center back leg seam. The seam was butted and sewn with whipstitches in silk thread matching the coral color of the stocking. The sole of each foot was knitted from the heel in a separate operation and seamed along the sides of the foot. This technique created a triangular shape at the ankles. The stocking top is finished with a ⅞" (2.2 cm) welt.

Left: *Stocking, frame-knitted in silk with contrasting decorative clocks at the ankles.*

Woman's shoe and embellished stocking, from Diderot's Encyclopédie.

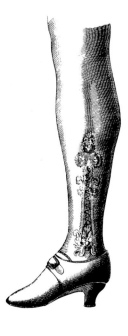

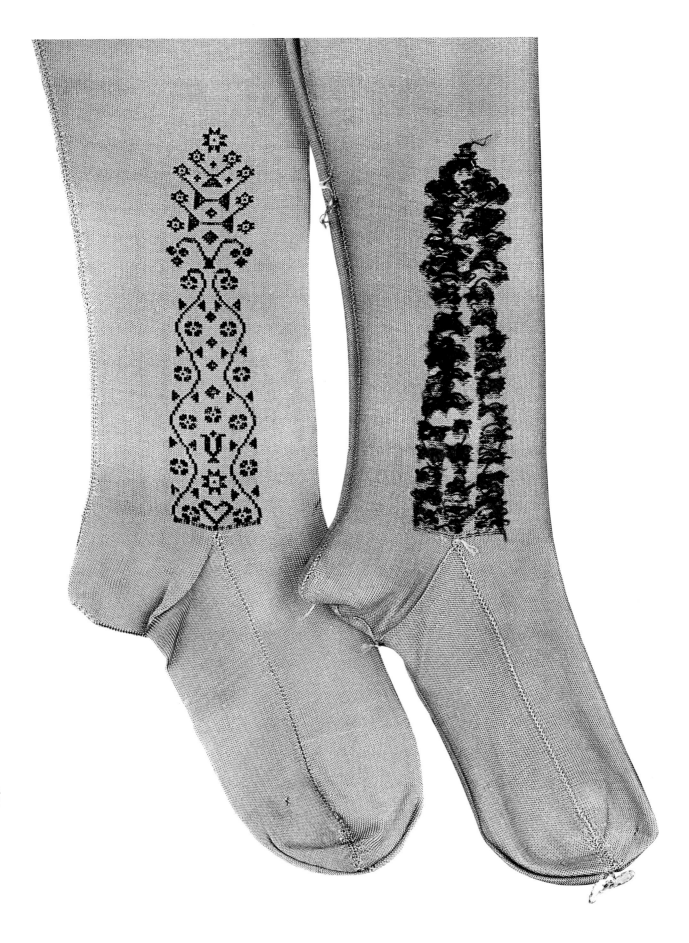

*Silk knitted stockings
with contrasting clocks.
One stocking is turned
inside out to show the
back of the decoration.*

Decoration: The stockings are embellished on both inner and outer ankles with a scrolling floral pattern in blue silk. The blue silk threads were knitted into the foundation stitches, resulting in an appearance similar to *duplicate stitch* embroidery. This technique was called *plating.*

1975-182

60   50   40   30   20   10   cm 0

30

24

18

12

Assembled
Stocking

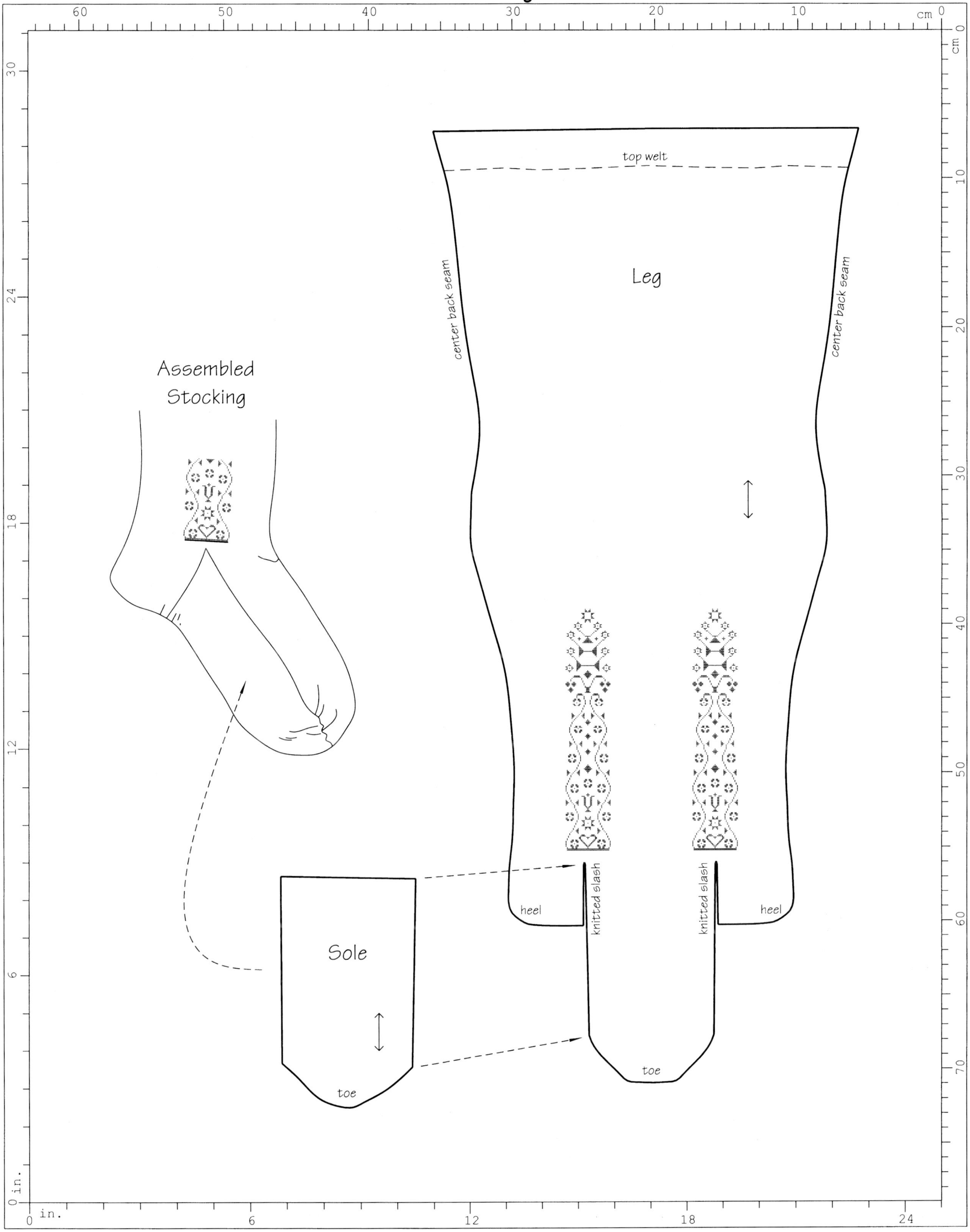

Sole

toe

Leg

top welt

center back seam

center back seam

heel

knitted slash

knitted slash

heel

toe

in.

0 in.

0   6   12   18   24

Pattern of Stocking Clocks

More about the stocking frame

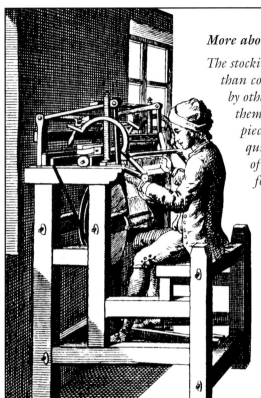

The stocking frame was a complicated apparatus that produced knitted goods more efficiently than could be done by hand. The frame was invented in 1589 by William Lee and improved by others over the next three hundred years. Male framework knitters, who had organized themselves into a guild as early as 1664, made stockings and other items of clothing as flat pieces that were then seamed together by female workers. Each frame-knit stocking required two pieces. The leg was shaped with curves to fit the bulge of the calf and the taper of the ankle; the curved edges became the center back seam. A separate small piece formed the sole of the foot.

By 1750 there were an estimated fourteen thousand stocking frames in England that produced items for use at home and for export to the American colonies. When Americans sought to assert their independence from British political domination and imported goods, they established stocking manufactories in their own towns and cities. In Williamsburg, Virginia, in 1773, a firm of stocking weavers urged people to bring their own spun cotton or linen to be made up into stockings, adding, "Those [stockings] that have been made are judged to be equal, nay superiour, to Needle knit." In 1775 Robert Carter of Nomini Hall set up several stocking frames on one of his Virginia plantations; Carter's operation continued after the Revolution ended.

Despite the success of stocking frames, hand-knitting on needles never died out. In the illustration taken from Diderot's Encyclopédie, *a knitter sits at his frame as would a weaver at his loom.*

Holding up stockings

Stocking garters consisted of ribbons or other woven tapes that were tied tightly around the leg, either just below or just above the knee. Men sometimes held up their stockings with the tightly buckled bands of their knee breeches. By the early nineteenth century, garters with metal springs could be purchased. Rubber elastic was not yet available.

The woman in the 1735 print by William Hogarth is shown with garters above her knees. Her dark-colored stockings have decorative clocks and a hole worn in the calf. Hogarth uses the discarded stays to symbolize the woman's role as a prostitute.

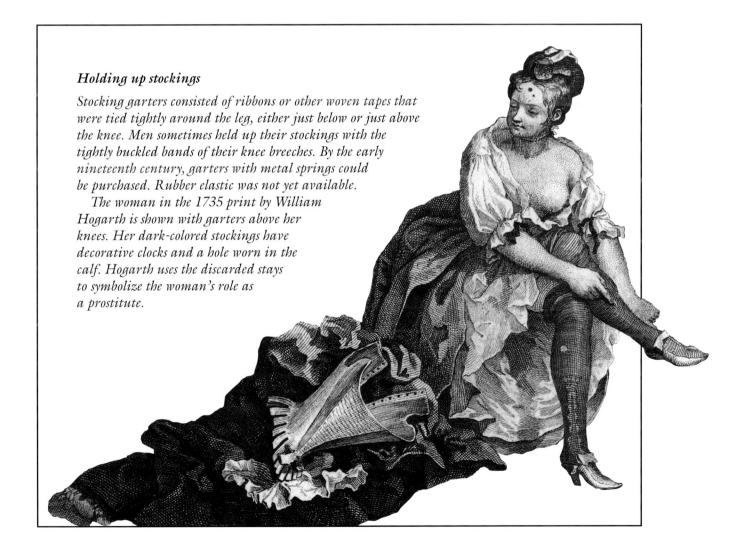

17
SUIT COAT, WAISTCOAT, AND BREECHES

England, 1765–1790

Beige silk woven with pink and green flower sprigs; silk and cotton-and-linen linings; linen interfacing; silk and linen sewing threads

Coat overall length, 41½" (105.4 cm); shoulder width, 13¼" (33.7 cm); chest, 37½" (95.3 cm)
Waistcoat overall length, 24½" (62.2 cm); chest, 35½" (90.2 cm); waist, 35½" (90.2 cm)
Breeches waist, 27–30" (68.6–76.2 cm); inseam, 16½" (41.9 cm); knee circumference, 12¼" (31.1 cm)
Silk selvage width, approximately 21" (53.3 cm)

Accession number: 1960-697, 1-3

During most of the eighteenth century, men's suits consisted of three pieces. Sometimes the three components matched each other; at other times they coordinated in material but had contrasting color or decoration. The knee-length coat had long sleeves, front button opening, pleats in the skirt, and deep pockets covered by shaped flaps. The waistcoat was worn under the coat, comparable to a modern vest. Waistcoats were very long early in the century but gradually had shortened to waist-length by the end of the 1700s. Breeches were knee-length pants worn with stockings that covered the lower legs.

The coat shown here is typical of a conservative man's suit coat from the period 1765–1790. It has a small standing collar; long, cuffed sleeves made to curve at the elbows; and a full sweep of skirt. Depending on the materials and trim, a coat of this pattern could be worn for formal or everyday wear.

The collarless and sleeveless waistcoat has twelve fabric-covered buttons down the front, and working pockets hidden by shaped pocket flaps. The primary silk textile of the fronts matches that of the coat and breeches, but the back is a double layer of plain, white, napped cotton-and-linen. Because waistcoats were covered by suit coats, the backs frequently were made of less expensive material.

The breeches have a generous seat gathered to a wide waistband and splayed legs ending at the knees. The fall front (opening) was popular during the second half of the eighteenth century, when waistcoats were short enough to reveal the front of the breeches. For an earlier style of breeches, see number 18.

Suit coat and waistcoat shown with reproduction lace ruffles. The sleeves are cut to bend over the elbows.

Materials

This suit is made of silk woven with a small spotted pattern of flowers in supplementary wefts carried across from selvage to selvage. Small-scale patterns like this one were especially favored for men's suitings. The coat and waistcoat have linings of ribbed silk. The coat has nonwoven bast fiber padding in the chest. All three pieces utilize napped, plain-woven cotton-and-linen as secondary lining materials, and all have interfacings of plain-woven brown and natural linens. The suit is stitched with both silk and linen threads.

Change over Time

The suit has no evidence of alterations or later repairs. The silk linings of both the coat and waistcoat have holes that reveal the interfacings and padding. There are a few stains throughout.

Coat Construction

Stitching: The coat was constructed with backstitches, running stitches, *point à rabattre sous la main* (see p. 8), and slanted hemming stitches. The primary seams are backstitched. The topstitching was done with close running stitches in light beige silk thread. Buttonholes and some lining pieces are sewn with linen.

Lining: The coat fronts and tails are lined with beige ribbed silk brought out to the edges, turned inside, and stitched with running stitches less than ⅛" (3 mm) from the edge. (The complete lining is illustrated on p. 8.) Although not consistent, in most areas, the running stitches go all the way through to the right side. Because the silk sewing thread matches the fabric perfectly in color, the edgestitching is scarcely visible. The pocket flaps and collar are lined with the same ribbed silk, which was turned under and sewn with slanted stitches that come through on the right side of the fabric parallel to the coat's edge, imitating running topstitching (*point à rabattre sous la main*). The upper back of the coat is lined with napped, plain-woven cotton-and-linen. This sturdy fabric was

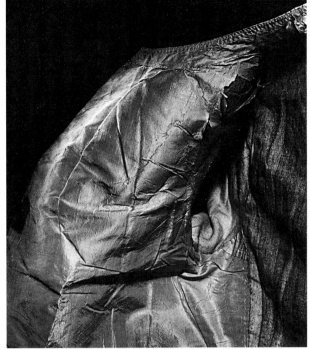

Interior of coat neckline, chest, and right armhole. The chest padding is visible through holes in the silk lining. The cotton-linen back lining is at right.

used instead of the expensive silk lining because it would not be seen when the coat was worn.

Coat Fronts and Interfacing: The fronts of the coat are curved to cut away below the chest. The prominent chest is emphasized with nonwoven bast fiber padding. Stiff linen interfacing supports the fronts from the shoulders to just above the hem. An additional narrow strip of linen interfacing was added to support the buttons on the right side.

Shopping for a suit in the eighteenth century

Suits were made by tailors, who measured the customer on the premises or kept the wearer's measurements on file. Many tailors worked in Williamsburg, Virginia. Jonathan Prosser advertised in July 1768 that he had studied a method for cutting out suits to save fabric. A frock suit for a middle-size man took only 3¼ yards of super-fine cloth, whereas a full-size suit made of narrower sagathy or duroy took 10 yards. Some fashionable men engaged in long-distance shopping and ordered their suits from tailors in London. Imported suits did not always fit as precisely as the customer desired, however. Williamsburg, Virginia, neighbors Robert Carter and George Wythe used the same London tailor, but Carter wasn't satisfied with the fit when his clothing arrived. He wrote, "The cloths you sent my Neighbour George Wythe fitted him much better than my last suit did me, for the sides of the Coat and Wastecoat were let out before I could wear them." Other men ordered from England all the materials for a suit, down to the buttons and pocket linings, and had them made up by a local tailor.

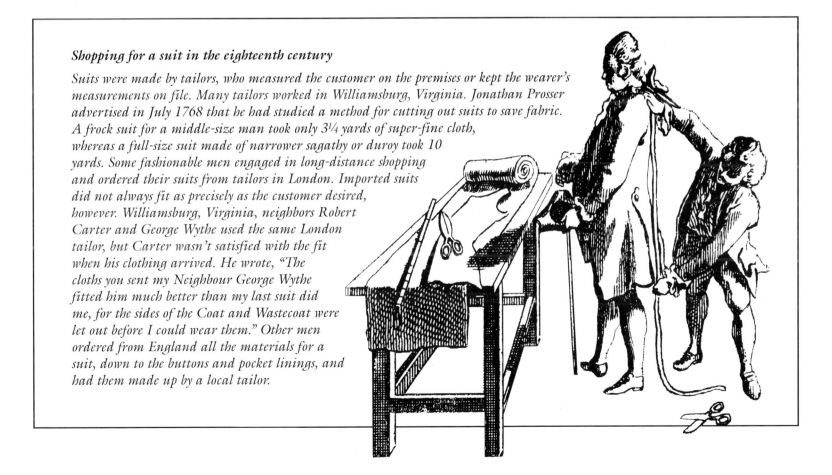

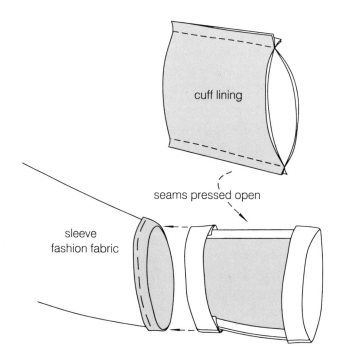

cuff lining

seams pressed open

sleeve fashion fabric

Collar: The coat collar consists of a narrow standing band, interfaced to give it body and attached to the coat with running stitches. The collar is lined with ribbed silk to match the other linings.

Buttons and Buttonholes: Because of the cutaway shaping, the coat must have been worn unbuttoned. Two sets of hooks and eyes, the first positioned 1/4" (6 mm) below the neckband and the second between the second and third buttons, are further evidence that the coat was not buttoned. The buttonholes are worked with linen buttonhole stitches. Only the top four buttonholes are cut open and functional; the remainder are decorative. All of the buttonhole stitches catch the coat front and the interfacing but not the lining. Behind each cut buttonhole the silk lining was slashed, turned under, and hemmed; this technique facilitated relining the coat as the lining became worn. The buttons at the coat front measure 7/8" (2.2 cm) in diameter and are covered with the suit fabric.

Sleeves: The sleeves and cuffs were lined and finished individually before being joined to each other with whipstitching and tacking. Each sleeve is made of two pieces—an upper and an under sleeve. The

The buttonhole on the coat and waistcoat are stitched with linen. The texture of the woven silk suiting is clearly visible.

sleeves are lined with napped cotton-and-linen. The lining is cut in the same shape as the silk fashion fabric for the sleeves but extends beyond the silk by 1/2" (1.3 cm). The extended linings were turned to the outside to enclose the raw edges of the silk, then basted in place. The raw edge of the lining was covered by the cuff. Like the sleeves, each cuff comprises two pieces. The two cuff sections were lined individually with ribbed silk, basted with wrong sides together, and treated as one piece when the front and back seams were stitched. The raw edges of the seamed cuffs were folded toward the lining and left unfinished, since they were hidden inside the cuff after it was attached to the sleeves. Each assembled cuff was butted and whipstitched to the finished sleeve along the bottom edge, then turned up and fastened in place with tacking and applied buttons. The sleeve buttons are stitched to the sleeve through all layers, including the sleeve linings. This method of cuff application made it easy to adjust the sleeve length by rolling the attached cuff up or down in position and tacking it to the sleeve along the upper edge.

Pockets and Flaps: The pockets are deep pouches, each made from two pieces of cream-colored cotton-and-linen fabric. The wearer put his hand through a slashed opening beneath a shaped flap to reach his pocket. The top 1 1/2" (3.8 cm) of each pocket was faced with silk lining material so that the cotton-and-linen pocket fabric would not show in use. The pocket openings have interfacing around them. To set in the pocket, the coat material was slashed and the raw edges were folded to the wrong side of the fabric toward the pocket and interfacing, then sewn with slip stitches and backstitches. The ends of the slashes were reinforced with buttonhole stitches. The shaped pocket flap was stiffened with plain-woven interlining, lined

Suit Coat

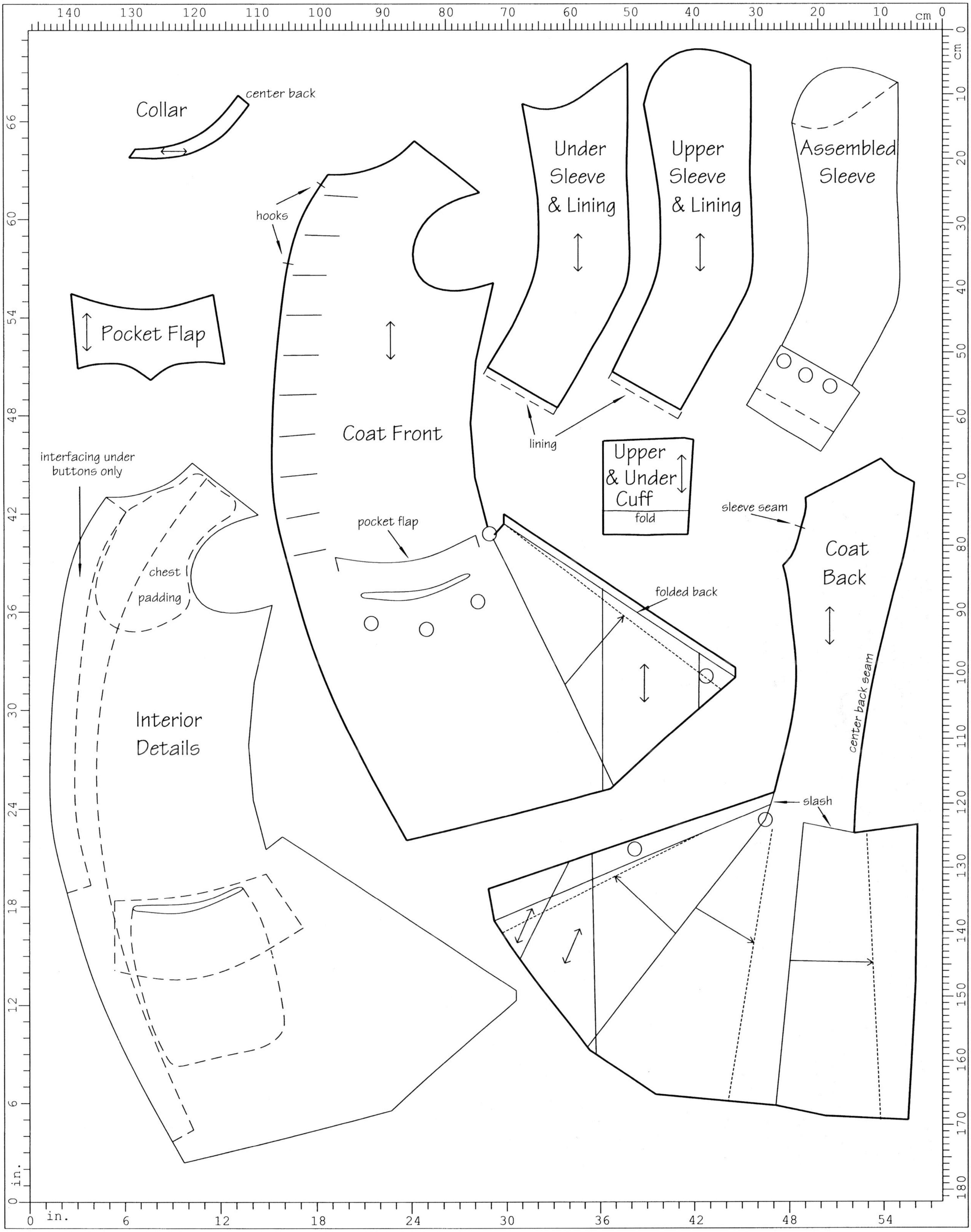

Collar

center back

Under Sleeve & Lining

Upper Sleeve & Lining

Assembled Sleeve

hooks

Pocket Flap

Coat Front

lining

Upper & Under Cuff

fold

interfacing under buttons only

pocket flap

sleeve seam

folded back

Coat Back

chest padding

center back seam

Interior Details

slash

The pattern of pleating the coat skirts. The pleats of the back and front sections were joined and topped by a button; see below.

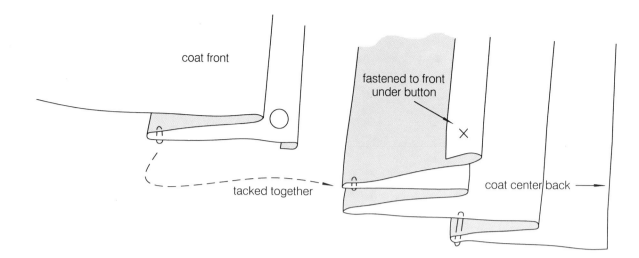

coat front

fastened to front under button

tacked together

coat center back

Left: *The left side of the coat showing the button-trimmed pleats and pocket flaps.*

Right: *Coat interior lining and pleats roughly tacked in place at the top.*

with ribbed silk, and sewn around the edges with *point à rabattre sous la main.* The upper edge of the assembled flap was stitched in place over the completed pocket opening.

Pleats: The side and rear pleats were folded and shaped after each coat piece was lined, treating the lining and fashion fabric as one for the pleating process. (See introduction, p. 8.) The tops of the pleats are coarsely stitched in place on the inside of the coat. Thread brides 8" (20.3 cm) up from the hem also tack the pleats. The pleats and long center back vent provided ease of movement and allowed a man to sit astride a horse.

Hem: The hem is turned up and covered by the silk lining, which was brought out to the edges and stitched with running stitches.

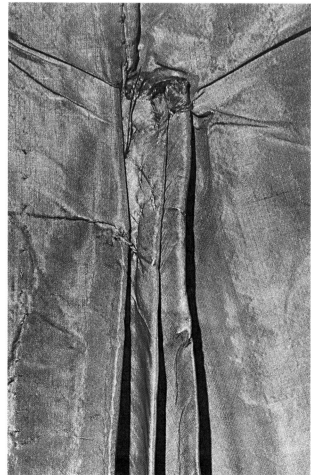

Waistcoat Construction

Stitching: The waistcoat seams are sewn with back- and running stitches. Other construction includes slip stitches and buttonhole stitches.

Lining and Interfacing: The front edges and skirts are faced with pieced fragments of the same ribbed silk used in the coat lining. The outside edges of the facings are sewn to the waistcoat fronts with slip stitches that came through to the top accidentally; they do not constitute deliberate topstitching. The remainder of the garment is lined with the same napped cotton-and-linen that forms the waistcoat back. Narrow strips of linen are used as interfacing on the front edges.

Edge Finish: The raw edges of the lining and outer materials at the armholes and neckline were turned toward each other and slip-stitched. A row of running and backstitches is worked about ¼" (6 mm) from the outside edge of the neck.

Buttons and Buttonholes: All of the buttonholes are cut open and functional. They were worked with buttonhole stitches through the primary fabric and linen interfacing but not through the silk facing. (See p. 82.) The facing was slashed, turned under, and hemmed around the worked buttonholes. Sewing the facing or lining in this manner—rather than working the buttonholes through the facing—made the garment easier to reline as the lining became worn, because the worked buttonholes did not have to be disturbed. The sewing thread used to attach the fabric-covered buttons was carried on the inside from button to button. The thread lies beneath the lining, indicating that the buttons were sewn to the waistcoat before the lining.

Pockets and Flaps: The pockets are made of cotton-and-linen. The openings are covered with flaps that

are interlined and lined with ribbed silk. The pocket area is trimmed with three nonfunctional buttons that are sewn to each side beneath the three points of the flaps.

Hem: The hem was formed by turning the outer fabrics and linings in toward each other and slip-stitching the edges.

Waistcoat, open to show the silk facing and cotton-linen lining. All of the buttonholes are cut open.

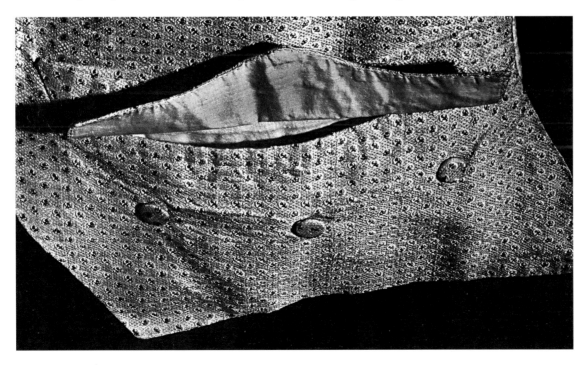

Left front of the waist-coat looking down into the pocket with the flap turned up. The buttons are decorative rather than functional.

Suit Waistcoat and Breeches

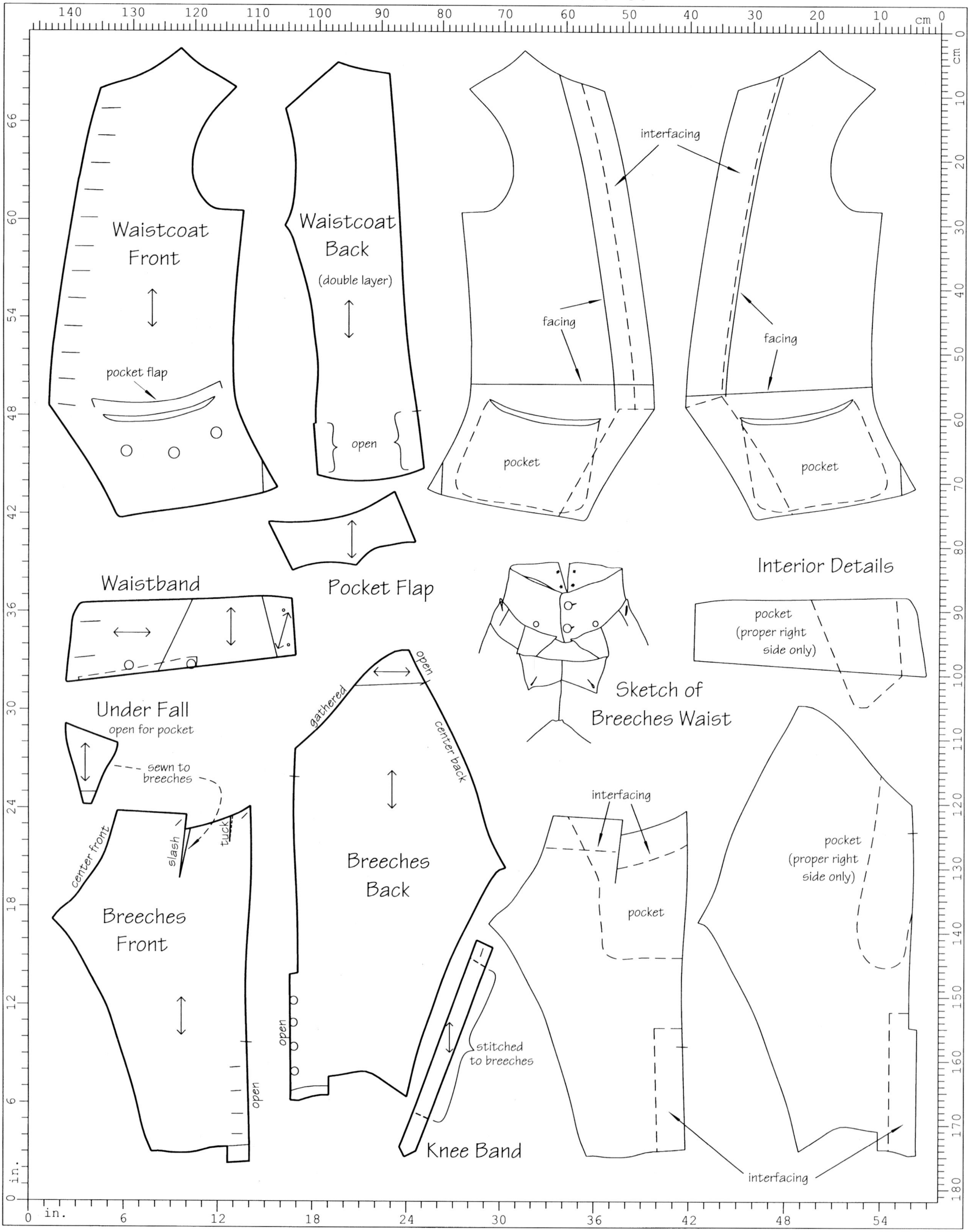

Waistcoat
Front

pocket flap

Waistcoat
Back

(double layer)

open

interfacing

facing

facing

pocket

pocket

Waistband

Pocket Flap

Interior Details

pocket
(proper right
side only)

Sketch of
Breeches Waist

Under Fall
open for pocket

sewn to
breeches

center front

slash

tuck

gathered

center back

open

Breeches
Front

Breeches
Back

interfacing

pocket

pocket
(proper right
side only)

open

open

open

stitched
to breeches

Knee Band

interfacing

Breeches Construction

Stitching: The breeches are seamed with back-stitches using two different kinds of linen thread (brown and natural.) The fall front is reinforced with an extra row of inconspicuous running stitches ³⁄₈" (1 cm) from the edges.

Waist and Closures: The breeches fasten with two large fabric-covered buttons on a wide waistband. The fall front attaches to the waistband with two smaller buttons. The flap was created by slashing the breeches fronts and stitching a triangular piece of fabric along one side of each slash. The top side of each triangle is stitched to the waistband. These pieces are hidden when the fall front is buttoned in position. The buttonholes are worked in button-hole stitches with pink and white linen threads that were loosely plied and treated as one thread. The two colors create a variegated appearance that blends with the colors in the breeches fabric. The back waist has a vent to allow for size adjustment by lacing through overcast eyelets.

Breeches with fall front opening. The waistband has adjustable eyelets at the back.

Baggy backs and splayed legs

Eighteenth-century knee breeches had very full, baggy backsides and splayed legs. The excess seat material was tucked or gathered into the waistband. Although such breeches do not conform to modern body aesthetics, they were absolutely essential for ease of movement in a garment that was constricted at both the waist and the knees.

Extra fullness was required in the seat to allow a man to sit or squat. The full seat and splayed legs prevented the seams from ripping out when a man sat astride a horse. Knit fabrics or leather gave more ease of movement. As men's clothing evolved to a slimmer line at the end of the century, breeches also slimmed down, and these elastic materials gained in popularity.

Inseams: The inseams were stitched through folded edges, possibly to prevent the silk from raveling under stress. The cut edges were folded with wrong sides together, and the inseams were backstitched through all four layers. (See sketch.)

Pockets: There are four pockets. Two deep pockets are located at the side fronts and hidden beneath buttoned flaps. A long, narrow pocket was worked in the seam at the right hip, and a smaller watch pocket was inserted into the right waistband.

Lining and Interfacing: The full lining of napped cotton-and-linen was cut to the plan of the breeches, turned under, and sewn around the outside edges of the waistband and fall using slip stitches and *point à rabattre sous la main.* The leg linings hang loose from the waistband and fall and are not caught into the seams, except at the knee placket. The linings are also loose at the knee bands; the raw edges are finished with blanket stitch to prevent raveling. Interfacings give extra body to the waistband, at the top edges of the fall front, and at the knee plackets.

Knee Openings: The breeches have buttoned plackets at the knees and narrow knee bands intended to be buckled tightly around the leg below the knees. The knee bands were cut on the bias, providing some ease and stretch. The bands are lined with cotton-and-linen. The knee placket buttonholes are worked through the breeches lining with buttonhole stitches. A section of silk selvage shows at the knee buttons; no attempt was made to turn it under where it meets the lining. ❦

Proper right front of breeches showing the waistband and, from left to right, inseam pocket, buttoned pocket, and fall front.

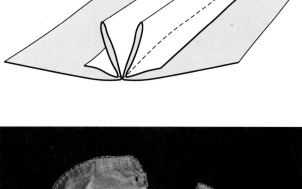

Method of sewing the inseams through two layers of the textile.

Right: *The proper left knee and knee band, seen from the back.*

Breeches waistband showing the watch pocket, back vent, and full lining.

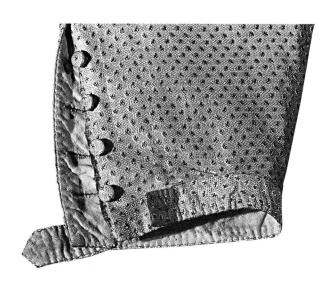

Coat and waistcoat no. 17.

Detail of pocket, waistcoat no. 17.

*Detail of textile, selvage, and buttons
on knee placket, breeches no. 17.*

Cloak no. 21.

Detail of neck and center back seam, cloak no. 21.

Interior, coat no. 19, showing linings and chest padding.

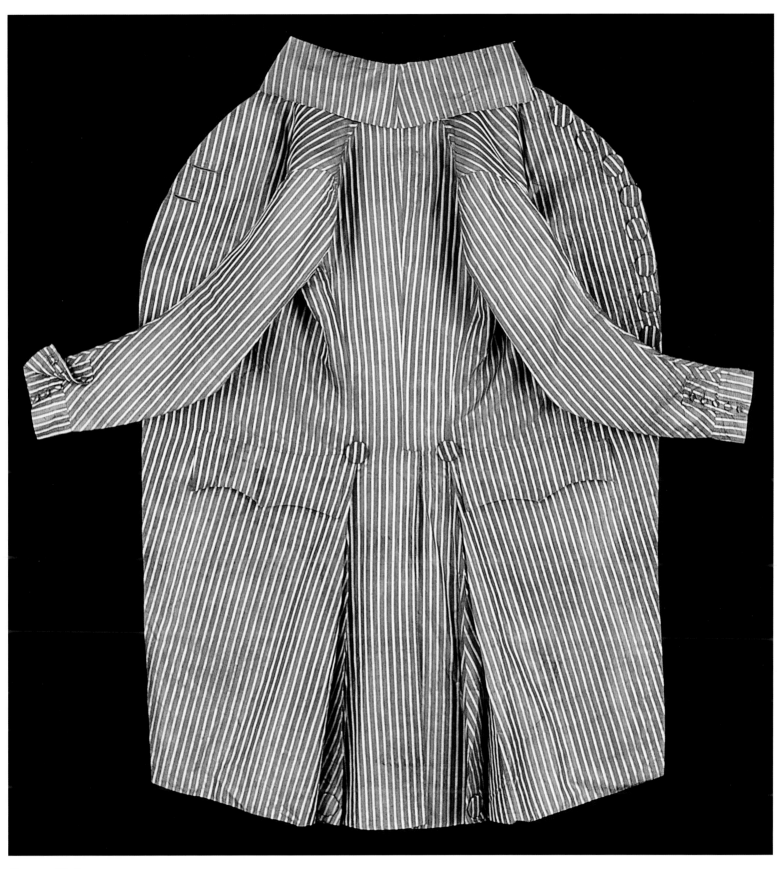

Coat no. 19, shown open.

Left front waistband and pockets, breeches no. 18.

Buttonholes and embroidery, waistcoat no. 20.

Waistcoat no. 20.

Cap no. 25.

🐝18

BREECHES

Europe, 1750–1760

Green silk with self-color woven stripe; linen; linen and silk sewing threads

Overall length, 26" (66 cm); waist, 30–33" (76.2–83.8 cm); inseam, 14½" (36.8 cm)
Knee circumference, 13" (33 cm)

Accession number: 1994-186, 2

These breeches are part of a three-piece suit. The use of a buttoned placket without a fall at the front to camouflage the opening typifies styles worn during the first fifty or sixty years of the eighteenth century. Early in the 1700s, men's coats and waistcoats were long enough to cover their breeches. The shorter waistcoats and cutaway coats fashionable in the last half of the century made the breeches more visible, however. Breeches began to feature a fall front like that in number 17, which gave a smoother appearance to the torso.

Materials

The breeches are made of green ribbed silk patterned with warp floats to form a textured self-color stripe. They are fully lined with natural-color plain-woven linen that also forms the pockets. The stitching threads are linen and silk. The buttons are covered with the green patterned silk.

Change over Time

The breeches show the effects of wear and age. Some buttons are missing, and stains discolor the seat. There are small holes in the silk and a patch on the crotch lining. Crudely constructed buckled tabs are sewn to the back vent, but the original adjustment was through lacing eyelets.

Green silk breeches from a three-piece suit. They have a fly front that closes with two buttons.

More about covered buttons

Many garments utilized buttons covered with matching fabric. A circle of textile was gathered around the edge and stretched over a button form made of wood, bone, or other stiff material. The fabric was drawn in at the back and tied off. Diderot shows these steps (left). A thread shank fastened the button to the garment. Men's suits required a great number of buttons of several different sizes. A typical pair of breeches required fourteen to eighteen buttons alone. Suit number 17 has a total of sixty buttons, all covered with the suiting silk; the coat has twenty-eight buttons, the waistcoat eighteen, and the breeches fourteen. The breeches in this section had a total of seventeen buttons (two are missing). Those shown at the right are from its matching waistcoat.

Breeches

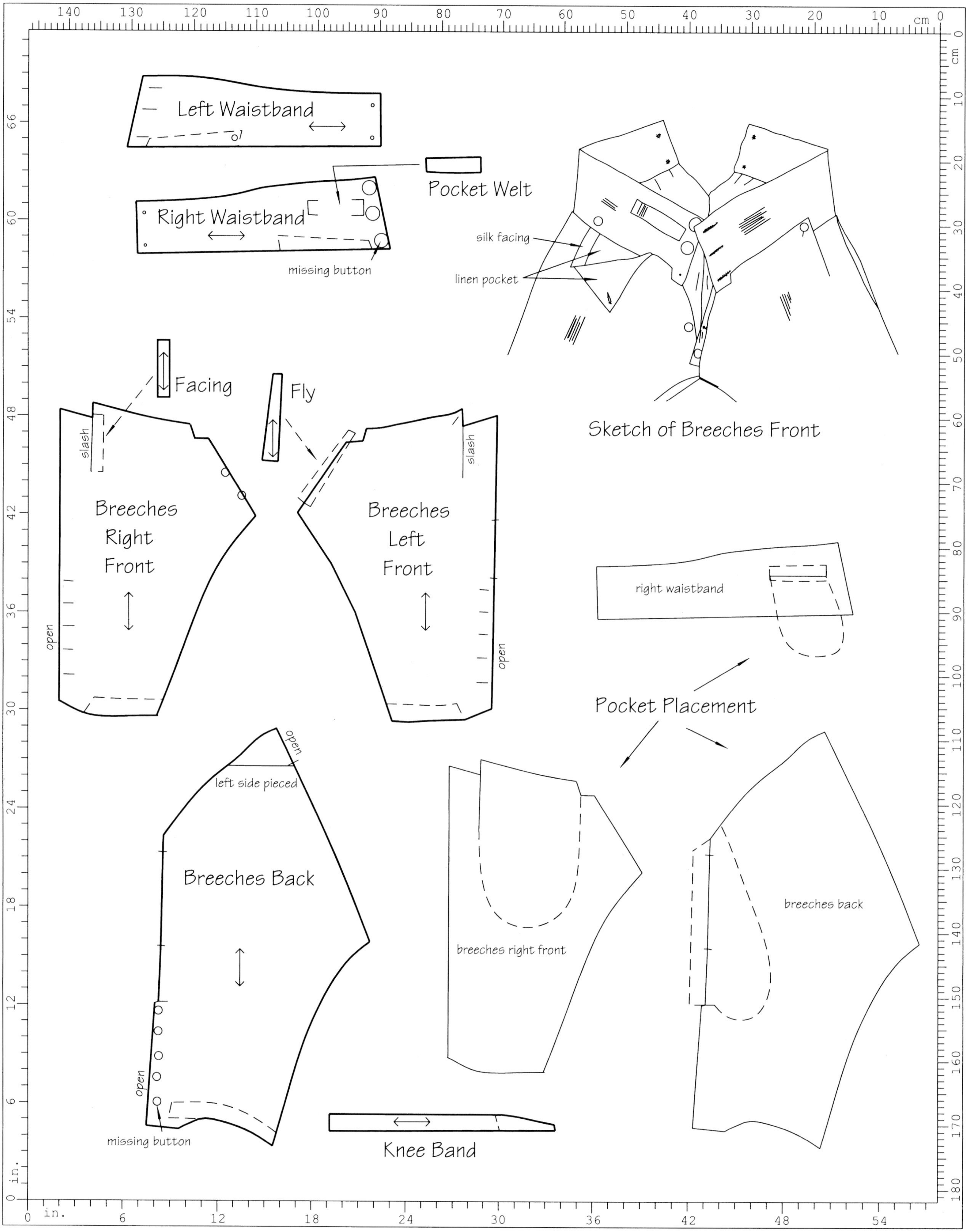

Left Waistband

Pocket Welt

Right Waistband

missing button

silk facing

linen pocket

Sketch of Breeches Front

Facing

Fly

slash

slash

Breeches
Right
Front

Breeches
Left
Front

open

open

right waistband

Pocket Placement

breeches right front

breeches back

Breeches Back

open

left side pieced

open

missing button

Knee Band

Construction

Stitching: The breeches seams are sewn with linen backstitches, leaving seam allowances of about ¼" (6 mm). Other stitches include buttonhole, *point à rabattre sous la main* (see p. 8), and eyelet. Green silk is used where stitching is visible.

Waist and Closure: The knee-length breeches have a buttoned waistband and front placket opening. The placket consists of buttons sewn directly to the right front and a separate fly extension with worked buttonholes sewn to the left front. The base of the placket is reinforced with a buttonhole-stitch bar tack. The fullness of the rear is gathered to the waistband. The waist is adjustable with a center back vent and lacing eyelets, later modified to a buckled tab at the center back. The eyelets are finished with overcast stitches.

Lining: There is a full lining made of linen, cut to the same pattern as the breeches. The lining was brought out to the edges and sewn with a stitch that resembles slanted hemming stitch on the lining side and running topstitching on the outside (*point à rabattre sous la main*). There apparently is

no interfacing; the linen lining itself is somewhat stiff and seems to answer the purpose of interfacing. The lining's fullness at the waist is pleated to the waistband, although the silk is gathered.

Pockets: There are five pockets made of brown plain-woven linen. A watch pocket with welt opening is set into the right side of the waistband. Two deep pockets are hidden under buttoned flaps. The flaps were created by slashing the fronts and stitching a narrow silk facing to one side of each slash. The pocket facing keeps the coarse linen pocket from view if the pocket gaps open during movement or sitting. The linen pockets extend to the upper edge of the opening, forming the flap lining as well as the pocket. The front pocket slashes are reinforced at the base with buttonhole-stitch bar tacks. Two more pockets are set into the side seams and directed to the back.

Knee Openings: The knees have five-button plackets and bands intended for wear with knee buckles. The knee bands are lined with linen. The knee bands were stitched to the legs after both bands and legs were finished and hemmed. 🪡

Breeches back, showing the full seat and splayed legs. The buckled tabs are later replacements.

19

COAT

France, ca. 1790

Striped silk; napped cotton-and-linen twill; plain-woven linen; plain-woven woolen; twill linen; silk and linen sewing threads

Overall length, 45¾" (111.1 cm); back shoulder width, 11⅝" (29.5 cm); chest, 40½" (102.9 cm)

Accession number: 1983-232

Coat made of silk striped with green, salmon, cream, and brown. Because of the cutaway style, only two buttonholes were used.

slimmer and more vertical and were cut away at the front to emphasize the chest. Although coat skirts retained pleats at the sides, they no longer flared out from the waist in a silhouette echoing that of women's gowns.

In spite of its fashionable appearance, this coat was not tailored with great precision. The two sleeve cuff plackets differ slightly in their size and button positioning. The coat has a variety of linings, padding, and interfacings, some pieced and apparently reused from scraps and leftovers. Even so, the stripes on the pocket flaps were carefully matched up with those on the coat's exterior.

Materials

The coat is made of fine silk of alternating ribbed and satin weave with green, salmon, cream, and brown stripes. The fronts and tails are lined with pieced scraps of the same silk fashion fabric. The sleeves and part of the back are lined with cotton-and-linen twill brushed to a napped surface—a textile probably called *fustian* in the eighteenth century. The linings were pieced from plain-woven

T his coat of striped silk has a high turndown collar, shaped pocket flaps, and ten large buttons down the front, although the cutaway is so exaggerated that only two of the buttonholes are worked and functional. The narrow sleeves curve over the elbows and end in buttoned plackets. The coat shows the evolution of men's clothing styles at the end of the eighteenth century. Coats became

Creating a fashionable shape

Today, most suit coats have pads that give the appearance of broad, square shoulders. Eighteenth-century coats also enhanced body shape, but with a different effect. Rather than perching on top of the shoulders, padding filled in the hollow of the chest and made it more prominent. This silhouette was especially fashionable in the last quarter of the century. The appearance of erect posture and a full chest was further enhanced by positioning the shoulder seams toward the back, rather than on top of the shoulders.

Collar

↕

center back

Under Collar ↕

Pocket Flap
(interfaced) ↕

Right Front

pocket flap position

pocket opening

Back

sleeve seam

Back Interior Detail

padding

interfacing to here

interfacing on right side only

Interior Detail

pocket

Cuff ↕ ○○

fold

Cuff Placket ↕

Upper Sleeve & Lining ↕

Under Sleeve & Lining ↕

Assembled Sleeve

slash

lining

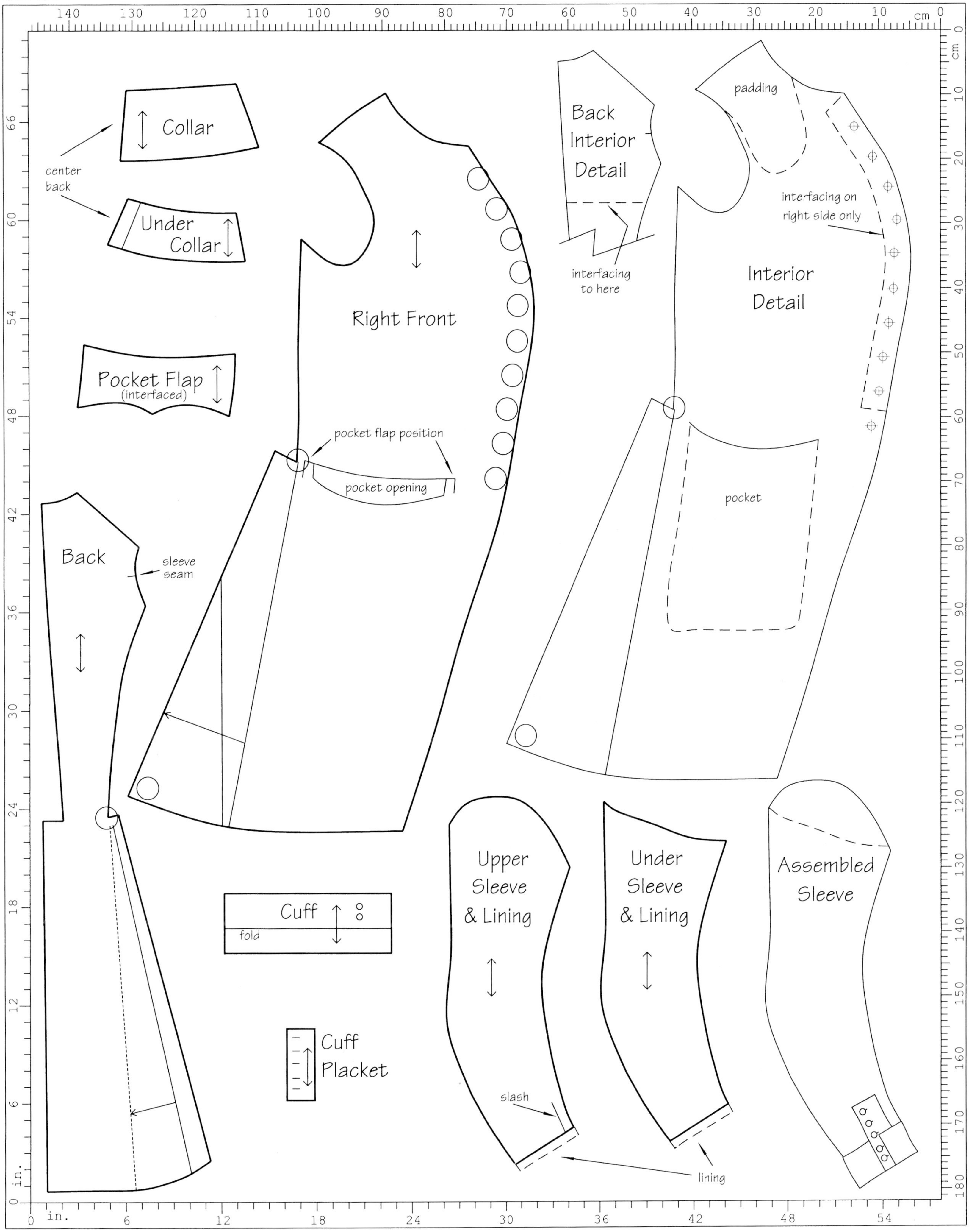

brown linen. The pockets are plain-woven linen and are partly faced with the striped silk. The lining of the upper collar, not visible when the collar is folded down over it, incorporates a fragment of blue striped cotton-and-linen textile. The chest is padded with layers of red, woven napped wool; linen; and silk. Interfacings are both plain-woven and twill-weave textiles, probably linen (they are visible only through backlight). The coat is sewn with silk and linen threads. Silk was used for all of the visible stitching.

Change over Time

The coat has not suffered significantly from wear and tear. A few interior seams have come unstitched, allowing one to see the interior detail and layers of padding. The pleats have lost their original pressed shape. The napped cotton-and-linen twill that lines the upper back and sleeves is pilled and abraded from contact with the clothing originally worn under the coat.

Coat right front collar, lining, and arm hole, showing padding through an opening in the seam. The sleeve lining is the same napped cotton-and-linen as the center back.

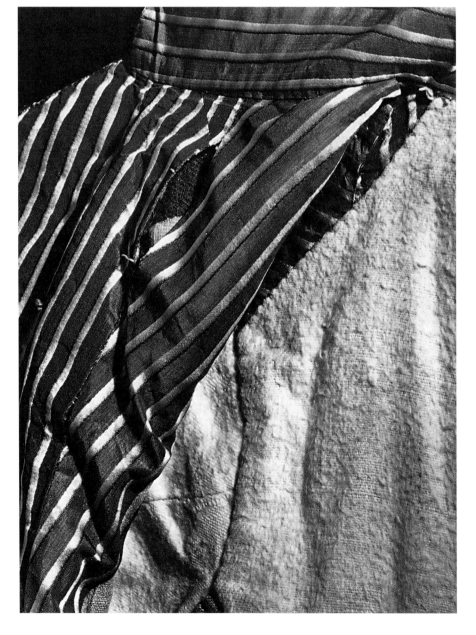

Construction

Stitching: The coat is seamed with backstitches using linen sewing thread; the seam allowances measure approximately ¼" (6 mm). Some seams were pressed open and some were pressed to one side. All of the raw edges where the linings meet the outer garment were turned to the inside and stitched with *point à rabattre sous la main,* a stitch that catches the lining from the back and simultaneously creates topstitching on the front. (See introduction, p. 8.) This visible stitching is worked with silk ⅛" (3 mm) from the edges. There is a center back seam, and a vented skirt opens almost to the waist. The center back seam of the fashion fabric is worked with 12 linen backstitches per inch (2.5 cm); the narrow seam allowances (³⁄₁₆" or about 5 mm) were pressed open and overcast with linen.

Lining: The coat is fully lined. The fronts, tails, and under collar are lined with the same striped silk used for the outer garment, cut to the same pattern and brought out to the edges. Some of the linings were pieced extensively from scraps. Under the arms and near the right pleats, the lining was pieced with brown plain-woven linen. The center back and sleeves are lined with yet another textile, a napped cotton-and-linen twill.

Interfacing and Padding: The coat has multiple layers of miscellaneous padding in the chest. Another layer of unidentified fabric interfaces the shoulders at the back. Light interfacings support the under collar, the right front edge, and the pocket flaps. The stiffening material in the under collar is woven in twill weave, and the remainder of the interfacings are plain-woven. (Because of the coat's fine condition, most interfacings are visible only through backlight, and their fiber content remains unknown.)

Collar: The high collar consists of a standing portion, or under collar, and a turned-down piece. Both the collar and under collar are seamed down the center back and lined with pieced scraps of silk and cotton-and-linen twill. The under collar has twill-weave interfacing.

Buttons and Buttonholes: The coat opens down the front and has large self-covered buttons that measure 1³⁄₈" (3.5 cm) in diameter. Only the third and fourth buttons have corresponding buttonholes; the remaining buttons are decorative.

Sleeves: The two-piece sleeves were set in without any gathers or pleats at the cap. On the interior, the coat lining was brought over the sleeve linings and sewn with slanted hemming stitches. The sleeves end with plackets at the wrist, buttoned with five ½" (1.3 cm) diameter buttons through functional worked buttonholes. Each sleeve has a narrow cuff that is stitched down with running stitches over the

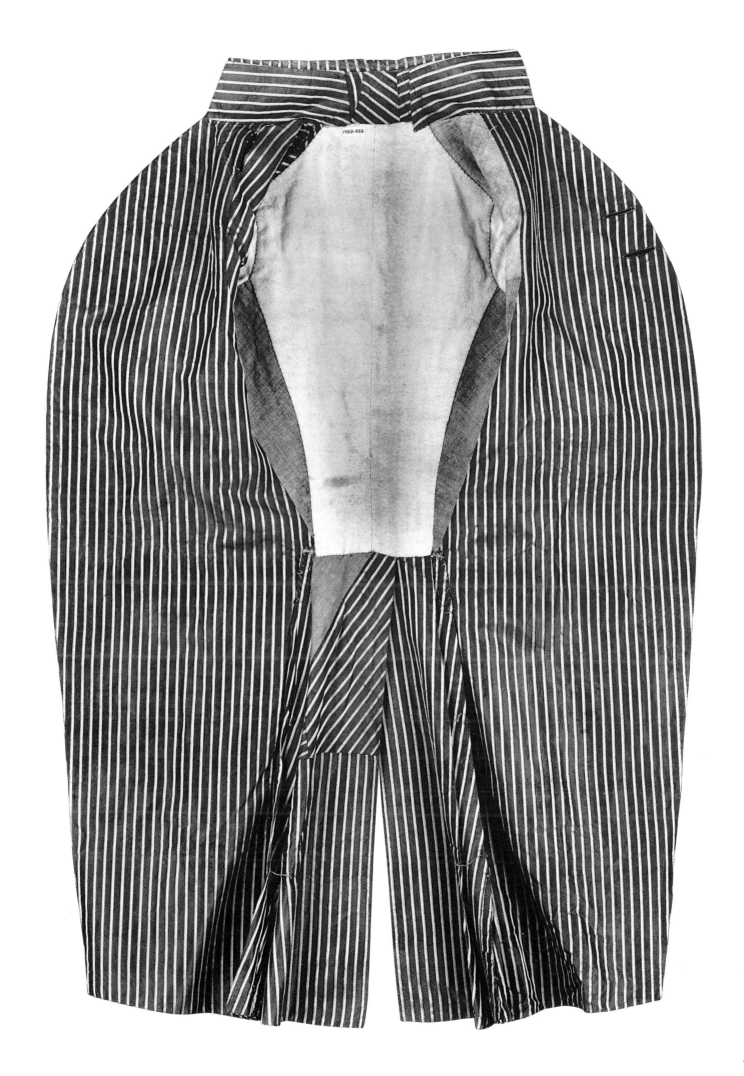

Right: *Pleating pattern
of the coat skirts with
lining side shaded.
Thread tacks and
buttons hold the pleats
in place.*

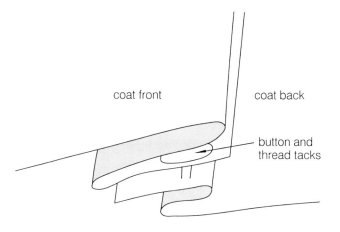

*Cuff and buttoned
placket on left sleeve.*

interfaced with an unknown material and lined with
striped silk.

Pleats: The skirts were pleated at the sides. The lining and outer fabric were treated as one for the
pleating process. That is, the skirts were first lined,
then pleated. (See introduction, p. 8.) The pleats
are stitched roughly on the interior about 3"
(7.6 cm) down from the top. The front and back
pleats are held together by thread brides ranging
from 1" to 1¼" (2.5 to 3.2 cm) long, located
about 7½" (19 cm) above the hem. In addition,
buttons sewn on the outside at the top and bottom
of the pleats hold the pleats in place.

Hem: The coat's bottom hem is worked through
both the lining and fashion fabric with running
stitches. The raw edges were turned to the inside
and stitched together less than ⅛" (3 mm) from
the edge. 🧵

placket. The cuff stitching goes through both the
sleeve and the sleeve lining. Although both cuff
plackets have five buttons, the cuff and button
spacing differ between the two sleeves.

Pockets and Flaps: Deep pockets of plain-woven
linen are partly faced with silk across the top of the
openings, keeping the coarser pocket material from
view when the pockets are used. The pocket openings are covered with shaped pocket flaps, which are

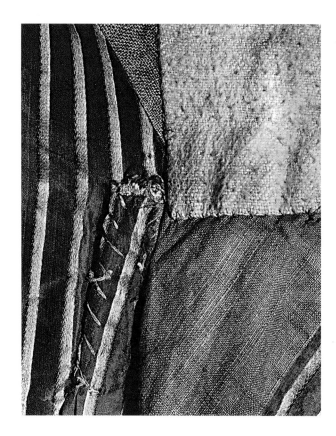

Left: *Interior of coat
pleats at the proper
right hip showing the
texture of the napped
back lining.*

Right: *Detail of coat
pocket flap and pleats
topped by a button
covered with fabric.*

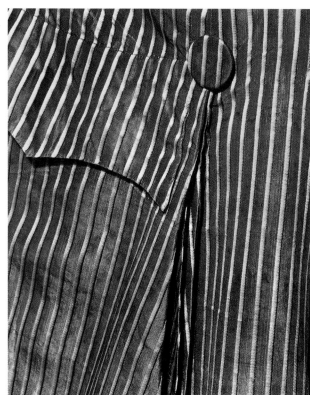

20

WAISTCOAT

England or France, ca. 1790

Blue, yellow, and cream silk satin; silk needlework; vellum or parchment spangles; cotton-and-linen twill; plain-woven linen; linen and silk sewing threads

Overall length, 23⅜" (59.4 cm); chest, 36¾" (93.3 cm); waist, 32" (81.3 cm)
Silk selvage width, probably 23½" (59.7 cm)

Accession number: G1989-433, Gift of Cora Ginsburg

variety, color, and pattern to an otherwise unembellished suit.

This example was professionally embroidered. The embroidered outlines for buttonholes appear on both the left and right fronts but are cut open only on the left side. The embroidered fabric may have been sold as generic yardage intended for waistcoats, or it may have been intended for use as a double-breasted garment. Instead, it was made up in a single-breasted style. On the proper right side, the buttons are sewn over the top of the uncut buttonholes. See page 98 for more about professional needlework.

Materials

The fronts and standing collar are cream silk satin with yellow, blue, black, and light brown stripes and a darker, shaded stripe border used as the center fronts. The silk was professionally embroidered over the woven stripes with silk floss, chenille, and punched parchment or vellum spangles (also known as *sequins* or *paillettes*.) Silk cord and chenille threads form decorative edgings. The collar, lining, back, and pockets are heavy cotton-and-linen twill that is napped on the inside. The interfacing is plain-woven linen. The waistcoat is sewn with linen and silk threads.

Change over Time

The garment is very fragile. The holes and losses correspond to natural patterns of use. Wear shows at the neck facing, where a starched shirt collar would have abraded the more fragile silk, and down the fronts, where constant buttoning would have caused stress. Ironically, the waistcoat's own construction has caused condition problems. The heavy, sized linen interfacing around the pockets weakened the silk from the back as the wearer's movements caused the two incompatible fabrics to rub against each other. Ink outlines for the embroidery are visible where the silk needlework has worn away. The side seams have large tucks where they were taken in early in the waistcoat's history or as part of the original fitting.

Left: Waistcoat embroidered with floss silk, chenille, and vellum spangles on striped silk.

French fashion plate, 1787. The man wears a striped waistcoat and coordinating stockings.

By the end of the eighteenth century, all but very formal suits had evolved in style, and waistcoats conformed to the new aesthetic. Changes in the cut of the suit coat revealed more of the waistcoat underneath. Instead of having long, full skirts or angled lines at the lower torso, waistcoats had straighter fronts that ended at or just below the waist. Pockets had a welted opening, rather than a shaped flap. Collars on waistcoats grew to reflect the new height of coat collars. Although embroidered waistcoats had been fashionable for years, they gained new importance as suit coats moved toward plainer materials for daily wear. A beautifully embroidered waistcoat gave

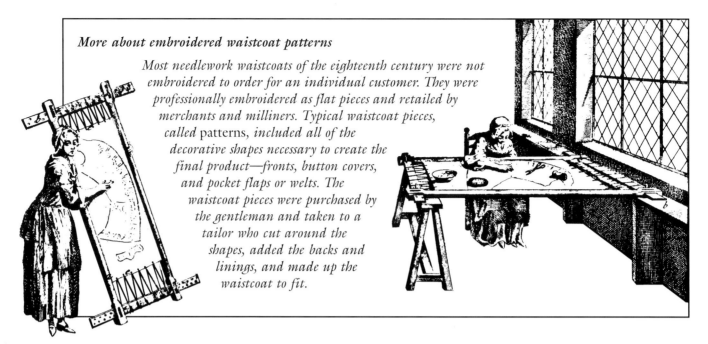

More about embroidered waistcoat patterns

Most needlework waistcoats of the eighteenth century were not embroidered to order for an individual customer. They were professionally embroidered as flat pieces and retailed by merchants and milliners. Typical waistcoat pieces, called patterns, *included all of the decorative shapes necessary to create the final product—fronts, button covers, and pocket flaps or welts. The waistcoat pieces were purchased by the gentleman and taken to a tailor who cut around the shapes, added the backs and linings, and made up the waistcoat to fit.*

Construction

Stitching: The waistcoat is constructed with back-stitches, running stitches, slip stitches, and slanted hemming stitches.

Embroidery: The embroidery combines silk floss, chenille, and spangles. It consists of isolated floral sprigs centered on the light stripes of the silk; the sprigs are worked in outline stitches, satin stitches, straight stitches, French knots, and applied spangles. The center fronts are embroidered with loops and trumpet-shaped flowers using spangles and satin stitches. Some of the embroidered motifs were cut through in the construction of the waistcoat, indicating that it was not embroidered *to form*, or to the exact shape needed for the garment. The buttonhole outlines were not finished or cut open where they were not needed but instead were left in place as part of the design. Buttons measuring 9/16" (1.4 cm) in diameter were covered with the silk fabric and embroidered with bursts of straight stitches. The button forms around which the silk is stretched appear to be bone.

Collar: The waistcoat has a modified standing collar, cut in one with the waistcoat front. The collar was given its standing shape by inserting a triangle of fabric over the shoulders and adding a separate back collar. The back outer collar is cotton-and-linen twill, cut in two pieces and lined with an unpieced strip of twill cut to the same size. The back collar was not cut with precision and appears rather lopsided.

Fronts: Striped silk faces the upper front and collar where they would fold back and be visible in use. Judging from the upside-down placement of the embroidered motifs, these pieces were made from the armhole cutouts. The embroidered fronts were appliquéd over a foundation of napped cotton-and-linen twill with running and slip stitches.

Left: *The lapels were worn folded back to show the striped and embroidered facings.*

Right: *Proper left shoulder and arm opening showing the inset triangle.*

1989-433

Embroidery Details

enlarged 5 times

1" (2.5 cm)

Waistcoat Front

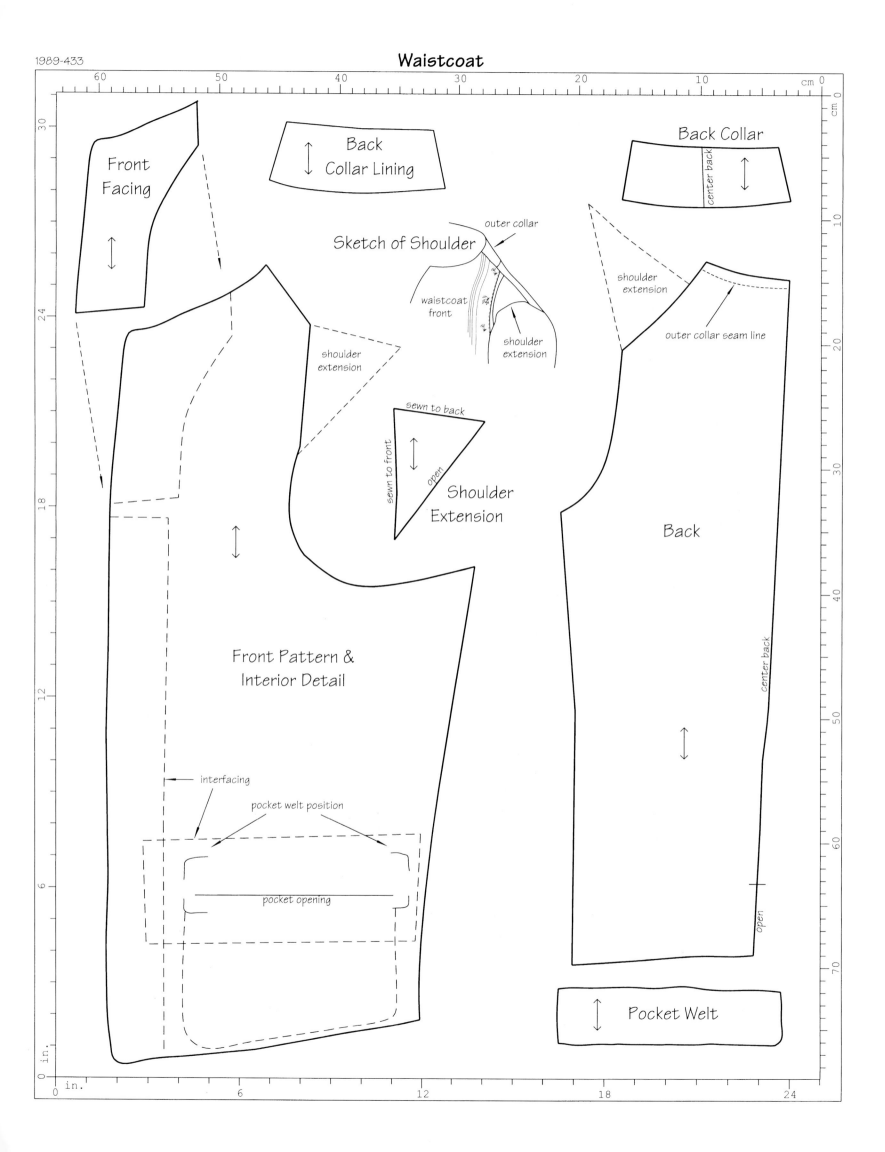

1989-433

Front Facing

Back Collar Lining

Back Collar

center back

Sketch of Shoulder

outer collar

waistcoat front

shoulder extension

shoulder extension

shoulder extension

outer collar seam line

sewn to back

sewn to front

open

Shoulder Extension

Back

center back

Front Pattern & Interior Detail

interfacing

pocket welt position

pocket opening

open

Pocket Welt

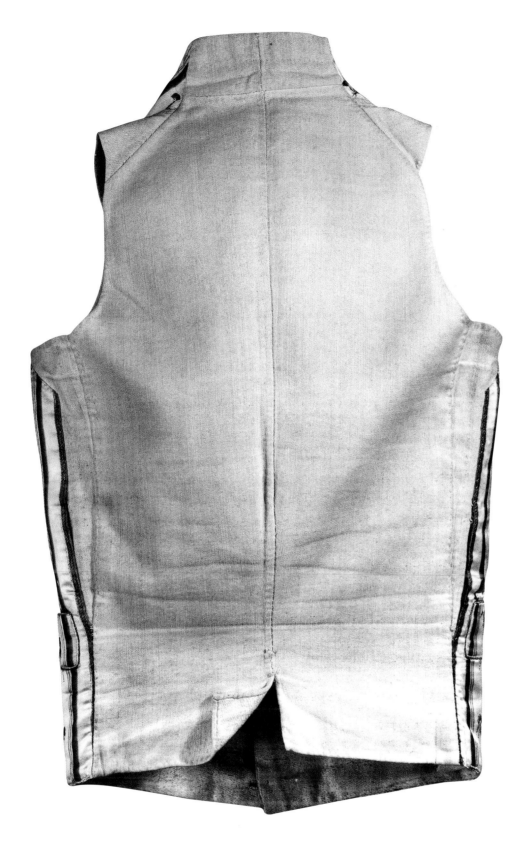

The waistcoat's back is a single layer of cotton-and-linen twill. The center back seam opens to form a vent.

Lining, Interlining, and Back: The napped twill serves as backing for the embroidered silk and as the front lining. The same napped fabric was used for the single-layer back. The joining seams are back-stitched and felled. Linen interfacings stiffen the fronts, the pocket welt, and the area around the pocket opening.

Edge finish: The outside edges where the silk meets the lining were turned in toward each other, slip-stitched, and covered with decorative cord and chenille threads couched to the edges.

Pockets: The pocket openings have a horizontal welt edged with couched cream silk cording and chenille. The pockets are made of the same cotton-and-linen twill as the back.

Hems: The hems of the back and armholes were turned under twice and hemmed with slanted hemming stitches. 🌷

☙21

CLOAK

New England, 1775–1790

Red wool, plain-woven and fulled; silk sewing thread

Overall length, 53" (134.6 cm); hem circumference, 180¾" (459.1 cm)
Wool selvage width (selvages cut), at least 54¾" (139 cm)

Accession number: G1956-213, Gift of Mrs. Reginald S. Graves

Although overcoats were available during the eighteenth century, some men wore full cloaks over their suits. A bright red cloak like this one didn't suit every man. Virginian Robert "King" Carter complained that the "fine gay cloke" he received from his English merchant factor was "fitter for an Alderman of London than a Planter in Virginia." Although he was one of the richest men in Virginia, Carter protested, "I love plainess and value my cloths more for their use than their finery." We do not know who wore the cloak discussed in this section, but it has a history of having been used in New England.

Materials

This cloak is made of slightly coarse plain-woven wool that was *fulled* (deliberately shrunk) to make it dense. The textile has about 36 threads per inch. It is sewn with pale yellow silk and is unlined.

Change over Time

The cloak is stained and worn from years of use. The wool was originally fulled but not as completely as high-quality broadcloth. This incomplete shrinkage has caused the cut edges to ravel slightly. A hole at the front neckline indicates the position of an original closure, probably a hook and eye.

Construction

Stitching: The cloak is sewn with backstitches, slanted hemming stitches, and overcast stitches.

The cloak's body is gathered to fit the rounded collar. The short cape over the shoulders is set back from the center front edges. The hooks are modern replacements.

Seams: The cloak body was made from two widths of wool approximately 54¾" (139 cm) wide. The selvages were trimmed off. The center back of the garment is sewn with backstitches and not pressed open. The sweeping semicircle is completed with small triangles of fabric stitched at the outside corners using backstitches, with the ⅛" (3 mm) seam allowances pressed open.

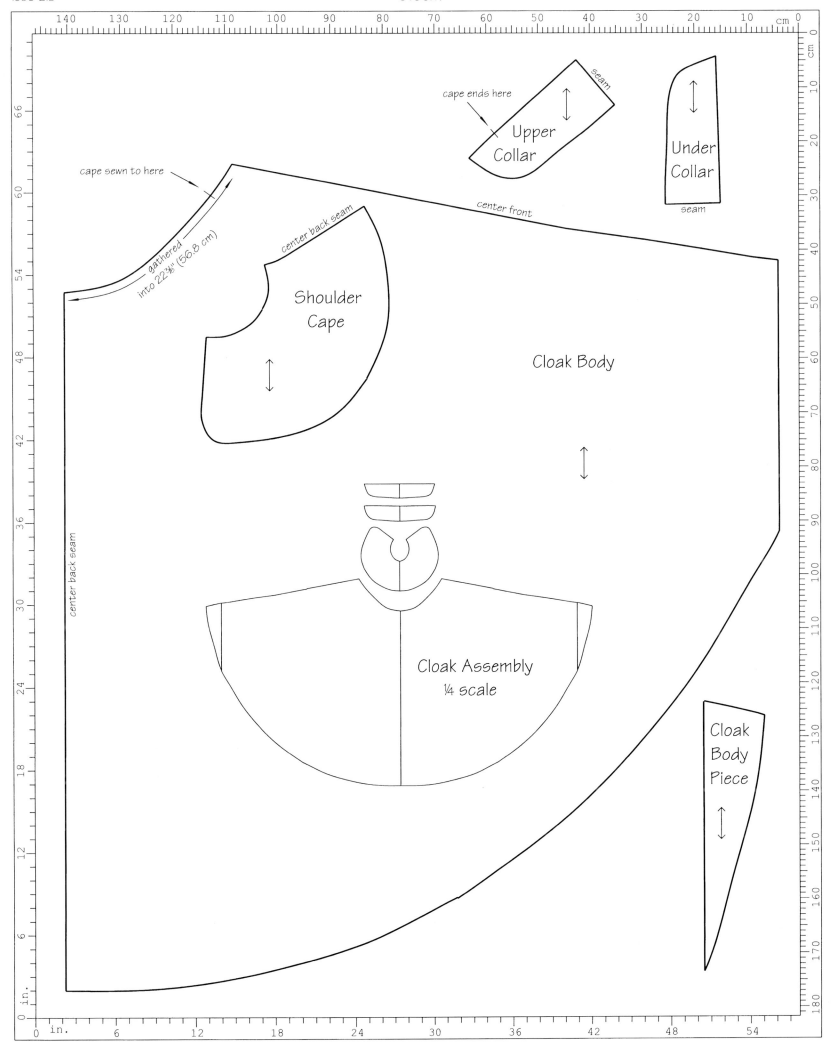

cm

cape ends here

seam

Upper Collar

Under Collar

seam

cape sewn to here

center front

gathered into 22⅜" (56.8 cm)

center back seam

Shoulder Cape

Cloak Body

center back seam

Cloak Assembly ¼ scale

Cloak Body Piece

in.

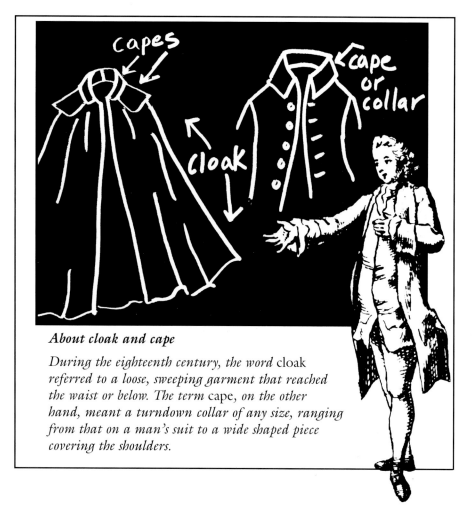

About cloak and cape

During the eighteenth century, the word cloak *referred to a loose, sweeping garment that reached the waist or below. The term* cape, *on the other hand, meant a turndown collar of any size, ranging from that on a man's suit to a wide shaped piece covering the shoulders.*

Fasteners: The cloak has a modern hook and eye at the top of the front opening. Loose threads suggest that another set of hooks was once sewn to the front of the cloak.

Collars and Cape: For the sake of simplicity, we will refer to the pieces as the *upper collar, under collar, cape* (the piece over the shoulders), and *cloak body.* The upper collar and under collar form a small double collar with rounded corners; the two collars were not sewn together around their outside edges. Each collar is made up of a single layer that is unlined and unhemmed. The upper collar was cut on the bias. The cloak body neckline is gathered slightly to fit the collar. The collars and cape were each applied individually in the manner shown in the sketch below. The under collar was backstitched to the gathered cloak neckline on the right side of the cloak body, leaving a seam allowance of about ⅛" (3 mm) standing upwards. The right side of the cape was placed against the right side of the cloak body, immediately beneath the under collar; it was backstitched and overcast to the cloak body. The cape covers the seam allowance when the cloak is worn. The cape is set back 2⅜" (6 cm) and does not extend out to the center front opening. Finally, the upper collar was laid over the other layers and stitched to the inside of the cloak's neckline with slanted hemming stitches.

Hem and Edge Finishing: All of the edges were cut and left raw and show some minor raveling.

Right: *The rounded collar is in two separate layers that were not stitched together around the outside edges.*

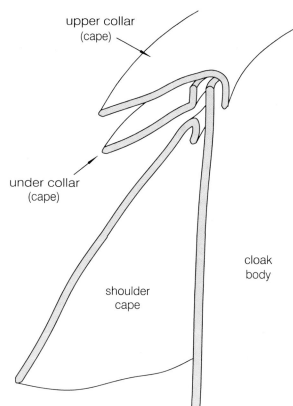

Method of assembling the collars and cape.

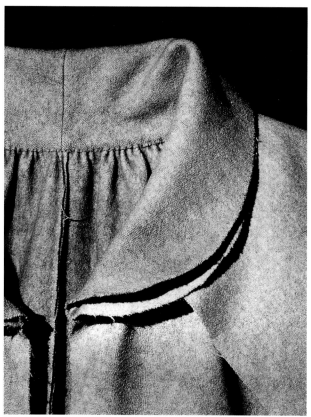

22

SHIRT

England or America, 1775–1790; repaired and remodeled later, probably 1810–1820

White linen; linen and cotton sewing threads

Overall length, 41" (104.1 cm); width including arms, 76½" (194.3 cm)
Neck circumference, 14⅛" (35.9 cm); chest, 58¼" (148 cm)

Accession number: G1974-268, Bequest of Grace Hartshorn Westerfield

White linen shirt. The neckband and cuffs were replaced in the nineteenth century.

Men wore their shirts next to the skin under their waistcoats, coats, and breeches. Although some men wore underwear such as special waistcoats or drawers, others used their shirts as their only undergarments. (See p. 110.) Shirts from the eighteenth century are extremely rare. Constant washing and ironing wore them out, and their plain fabric was useful for rags. This shirt was, in fact, repaired and remodeled in the nineteenth century. Shirts were very traditional in their construction and cut, and only the buttons, the width of the cuffs, and the cotton sewing thread suggest a later date for this one.

Materials

The shirt is constructed from three different qualities of white plain-woven linen, ranging from 40 to 80 warps per inch (2.5 cm). The replaced cuffs are finer than the rest of the garment. The linen of the body was evenly woven at about 54 threads per inch (2.5 cm). The shirt was sewn in the eighteenth century with linen and altered in the nineteenth century with cotton.

Change over Time

The shirt was altered in the early nineteenth century by adding new cuffs with mother-of-pearl buttons and reapplying the collar, possibly after turning or cutting down the original collar. The use of cotton sewing thread on the collar, cuffs, and repairs confirms the suspicion of alterations, since this kind of thread was not developed until the early nineteenth century. There are small holes, mends, and stains.

Workman in a shirt and breeches, from Diderot's Encyclopédie.

Shirt

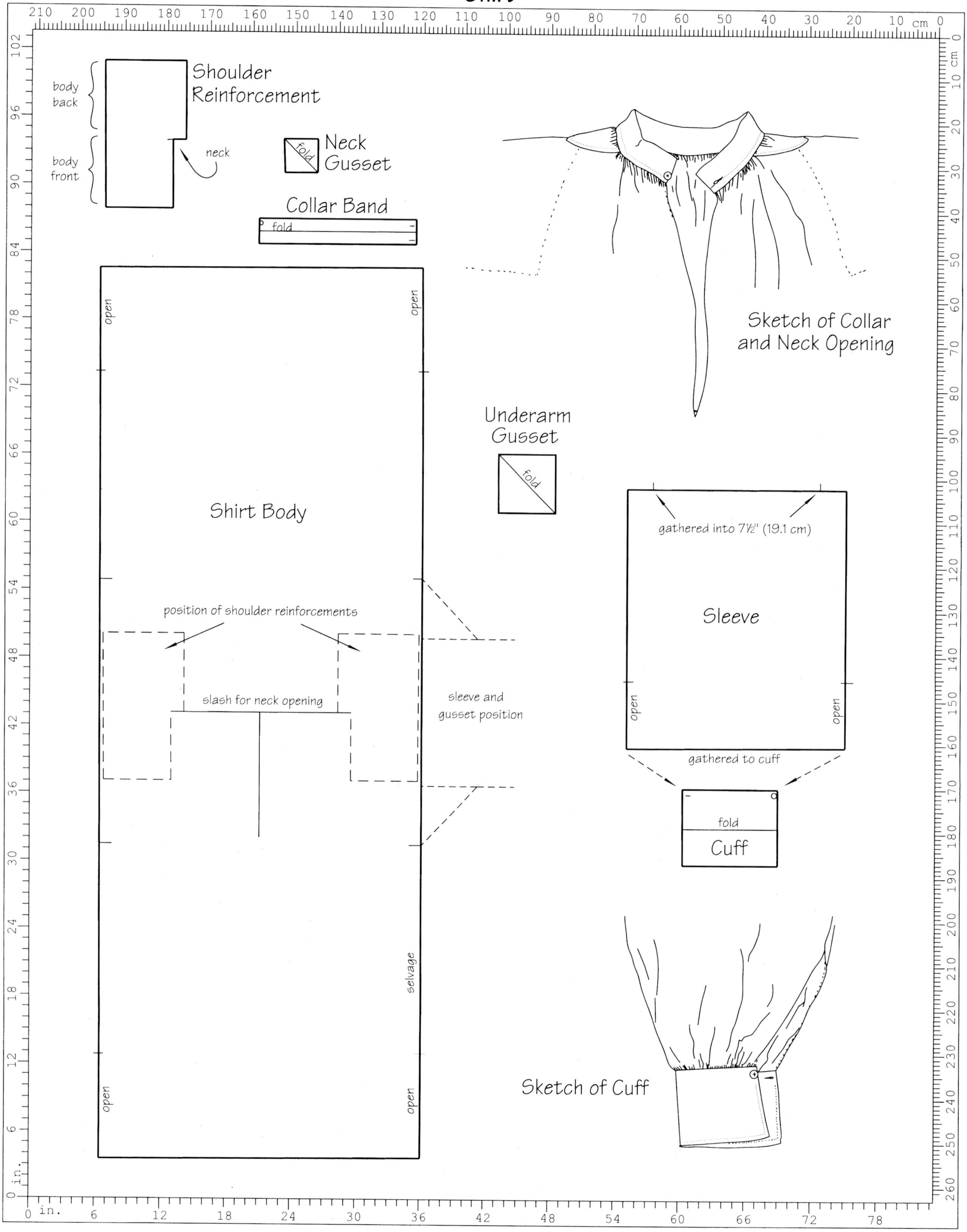

Shoulder Reinforcement

body back

body front

neck

Neck Gusset

fold

Collar Band

fold

Sketch of Collar and Neck Opening

open

open

Shirt Body

Underarm Gusset

fold

position of shoulder reinforcements

slash for neck opening

sleeve and gusset position

selvage

open

open

gathered into 7½" (19.1 cm)

Sleeve

open

open

gathered to cuff

fold

Cuff

Sketch of Cuff

Construction

Stitching: This shirt is a fascinating example of repairing and recycling expensive textiles, a history detected through microscopic analysis of the sewing threads. Typical of eighteenth-century practice, the body and sleeve seams and gusset topstitching are sewn with linen, but the collar and cuffs—parts that would have suffered the most wear over time and had to be replaced—are seamed and topstitched with cotton thread. These repairs and replacements suggest that the shirt was used over a long period.

Shirts of the eighteenth and early nineteenth centuries were usually made with close, fine stitching that would withstand laundering. This shirt was sewn with exceptional care. The seam allowances and hems measure only ⅛" (3 mm) wide, and all raw edges were carefully turned under and finished. The seam at the proper left body consists of selvages butted together and whipstitched. The cut edges of the opposite side are sewn with backstitches and felled.

Neck Opening and Collar: The front opening extends 10¾" (27.3 cm) down the chest; the raw edges are turned under and hemmed. A button-hole-stitched bride is worked at the point to reinforce the slashed opening. The bride appears to be a later replacement. The backstitching around the edges of the collar and neck gusset does not catch the linen on the back, indicating that it was done during construction or alteration, not at the end of the sewing process.

Sleeves: The sleeves are gathered to the shirt body at the shoulders and to the cuffs. The sleeve buttonholes are positioned on the front of each cuff. A mother-of-pearl button ⅜" (1 cm) in diameter is sewn to the back of the cuff with cotton thread. The cuffs are topstitched with backstitches.

Reinforcements: Reinforcement patches sewn to the inside at the shoulders are made of coarser linen woven about 36 by 44 threads per inch (2.5 cm), turned under, and slip-stitched.

Side Vents: The tails were vented by leaving the seams open 9¼" (23.5 cm) above the hems. The left vent has selvages as its finish, and the right vent has ⅛" (3 mm) hems.

Hem: The hem was turned under ⅛" (3 mm) and sewn with slanted hemming stitches. ✦

The shirt body was gathered to the narrow band collar. The slope of the shoulders was achieved with an inserted gusset.

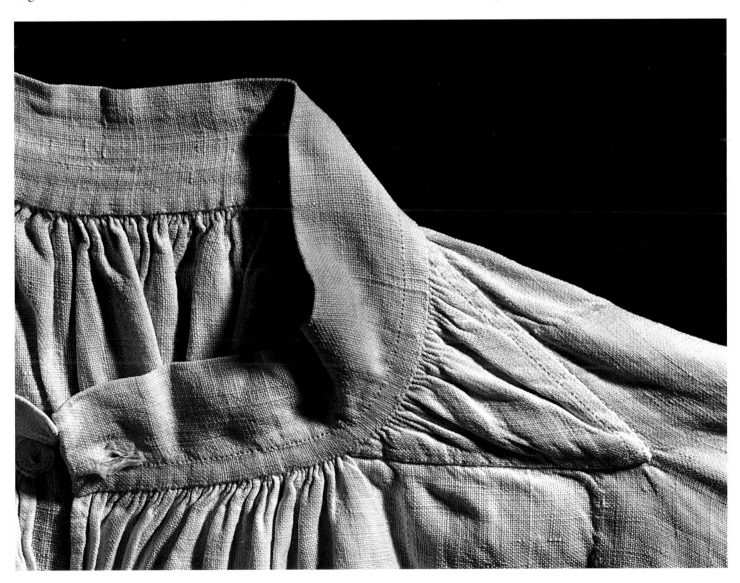

About cutting shirts

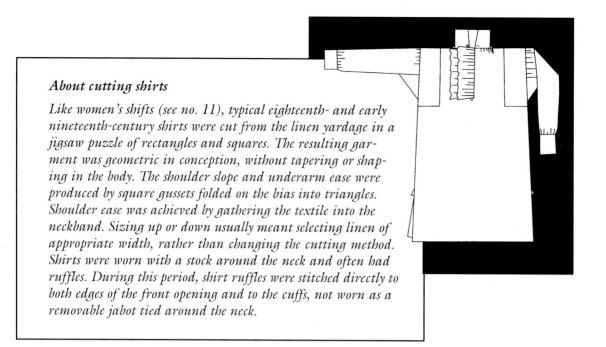

Like women's shifts (see no. 11), typical eighteenth- and early nineteenth-century shirts were cut from the linen yardage in a jigsaw puzzle of rectangles and squares. The resulting garment was geometric in conception, without tapering or shaping in the body. The shoulder slope and underarm ease were produced by square gussets folded on the bias into triangles. Shoulder ease was achieved by gathering the textile into the neckband. Sizing up or down usually meant selecting linen of appropriate width, rather than changing the cutting method. Shirts were worn with a stock around the neck and often had ruffles. During this period, shirt ruffles were stitched directly to both edges of the front opening and to the cuffs, not worn as a removable jabot tied around the neck.

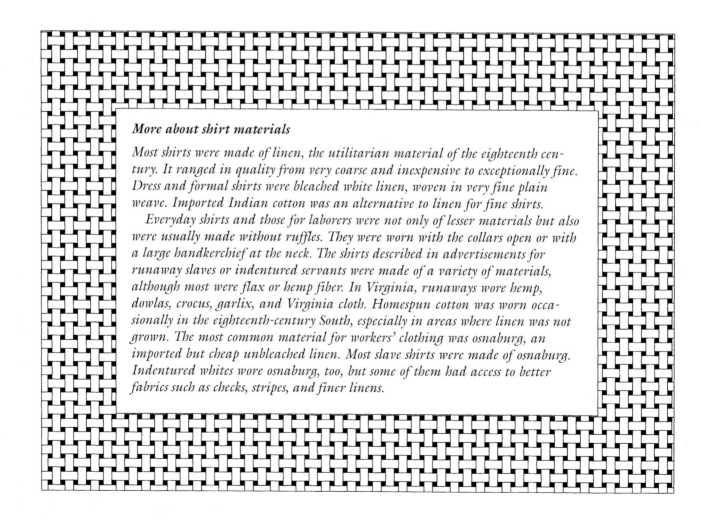

More about shirt materials

Most shirts were made of linen, the utilitarian material of the eighteenth century. It ranged in quality from very coarse and inexpensive to exceptionally fine. Dress and formal shirts were bleached white linen, woven in very fine plain weave. Imported Indian cotton was an alternative to linen for fine shirts.

Everyday shirts and those for laborers were not only of lesser materials but also were usually made without ruffles. They were worn with the collars open or with a large handkerchief at the neck. The shirts described in advertisements for runaway slaves or indentured servants were made of a variety of materials, although most were flax or hemp fiber. In Virginia, runaways wore hemp, dowlas, crocus, garlix, and Virginia cloth. Homespun cotton was worn occasionally in the eighteenth-century South, especially in areas where linen was not grown. The most common material for workers' clothing was osnaburg, an imported but cheap unbleached linen. Most slave shirts were made of osnaburg. Indentured whites wore osnaburg, too, but some of them had access to better fabrics such as checks, stripes, and finer linens.

🌶 23
UNDER DRAWERS

France, 1750–1800

White plain-woven linen; linen twill tape; bone button forms; blue silk marking thread; linen sewing thread

Overall length, 27" (68.6 cm); waist, 26½"–29" (67.3–73.7 cm)
Inseam, 21" (53.3 cm); knee band circumference, 12½" (31.8 cm)

Accession number: 1996-218

Construction

Stitching: All of the seams are sewn with back-stitches and felled, leaving no raw edges to irritate the skin or ravel during laundering. Other techniques include buttonhole stitch, whipstitch, running stitch, eyelet stitch, and cross-stitch.

Waistband: The drawers have a wide waistband fastened with two fabric-covered buttons, ⅞" (2.2 cm) in diameter, that button through stitched buttonholes. Each button is covered with a circle of linen that was gathered around the form, drawn in, and tied off on the back. (See p. 89.) The inner button forms are probably bone and are shaped like a flattened doughnut with a single center hole. The waistband lining was pieced from the same linen as the front. Around the perimeter of the waistband, the raw edges of the two layers were turned inside and whipstitched with linen thread. Two pairs of

Left: Front view of the white linen drawers.

Drawers waistband and front button opening. The initial is probably that of the owner.

U nder drawers were knee-length pants usually made from woven linen or wool flannel. When washed, linen becomes soft and comfortable, and drawers could be made more comfortable by finishing all the seams smoothly. Thomas Jefferson's drawers, in the collections at Monticello, have the seams turned to the outside, eliminating any ridges that might have irritated his skin. The under drawers in this section have flat-felled seams. They have two buttons at the waistband but no fastenings on the center front placket. The waist is adjusted by tightening or loosening laces through four center back eyelets.

Materials

The drawers are made of soft, white plain-woven linen and sewn with linen thread. The button forms are probably bone. Linen twill tape makes up the knee band and ties. The drawers are marked with a letter *T* worked in blue silk cross-stitches.

Change over Time

The drawers are patched behind the right knee with linen similar in quality to the rest of the drawers. Holes at the back of the left knee are mended.

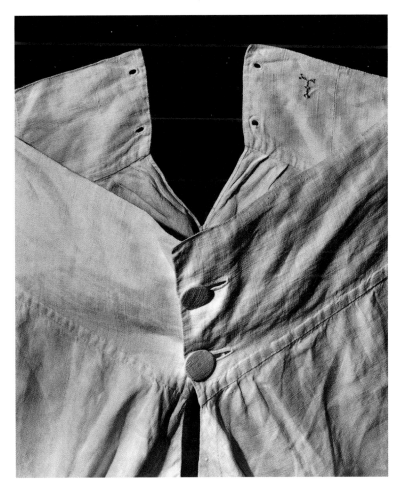

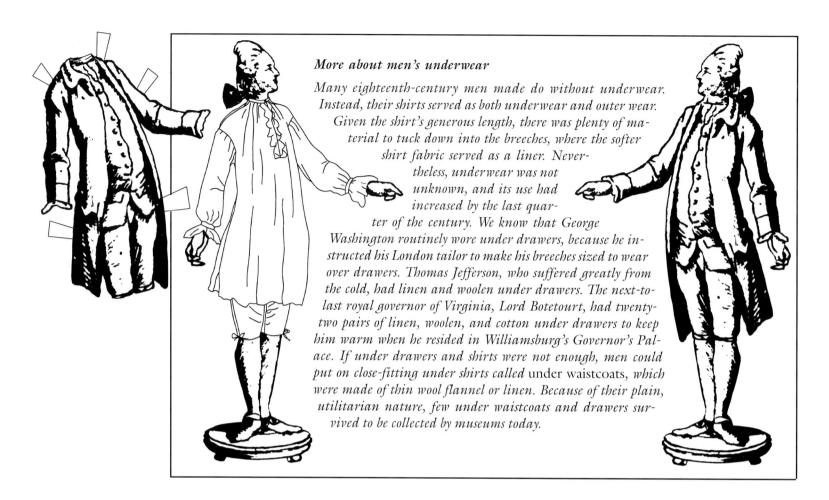

More about men's underwear

Many eighteenth-century men made do without underwear. Instead, their shirts served as both underwear and outer wear. Given the shirt's generous length, there was plenty of material to tuck down into the breeches, where the softer shirt fabric served as a liner. Nevertheless, underwear was not unknown, and its use had increased by the last quarter of the century. We know that George Washington routinely wore under drawers, because he instructed his London tailor to make his breeches sized to wear over drawers. Thomas Jefferson, who suffered greatly from the cold, had linen and woolen under drawers. The next-to-last royal governor of Virginia, Lord Botetourt, had twenty-two pairs of linen, woolen, and cotton under drawers to keep him warm when he resided in Williamsburg's Governor's Palace. If under drawers and shirts were not enough, men could put on close-fitting under shirts called under waistcoats, *which were made of thin wool flannel or linen. Because of their plain, utilitarian nature, few under waistcoats and drawers survived to be collected by museums today.*

overcast eyelets at the center back are intended for adjustment lacing. The letter *T* is worked with cross-stitch on the inside waistband.

Fly: The center front opening is finished with strips of ½" to ¾" (1.3 to 1.9 cm) wide self-fabric facing, with the right side of the facings stitched to the right side of the fronts. The facing was then turned to the back, and the raw edges were turned under and stitched down. There are no buttons on the fly.

Body and Legs: The full seat is pleated toward the center back seam and the front eased with four small tucks. The raw edges of the tucked body pieces were enclosed by the two layers of waistband and lining. The seam was then topstitched with 10 running stitches per inch (2.5 cm), positioned about ⅜" (1 cm) from the seam line.

Knees: Each knee placket facing is a rectangle of linen slashed up 4¼" (11.4 cm) and stitched to the knee opening. The right knee facing was pieced. The raw edges of the leg openings were turned under and covered with white linen twill tape sewn to the back. Lengths of the same linen twill tape are stitched to the knee openings for ties that average 16" (40.6 cm) in length. The proper right leg has a large patch behind the knee. The patch is about 5" by 6" (12.7 by 15.2 cm) and is stitched with running stitches and felled. 🪡

Right: *Proper right knee placket. White linen twill tape is sewn to the back side and forms ties.*

Under Drawers

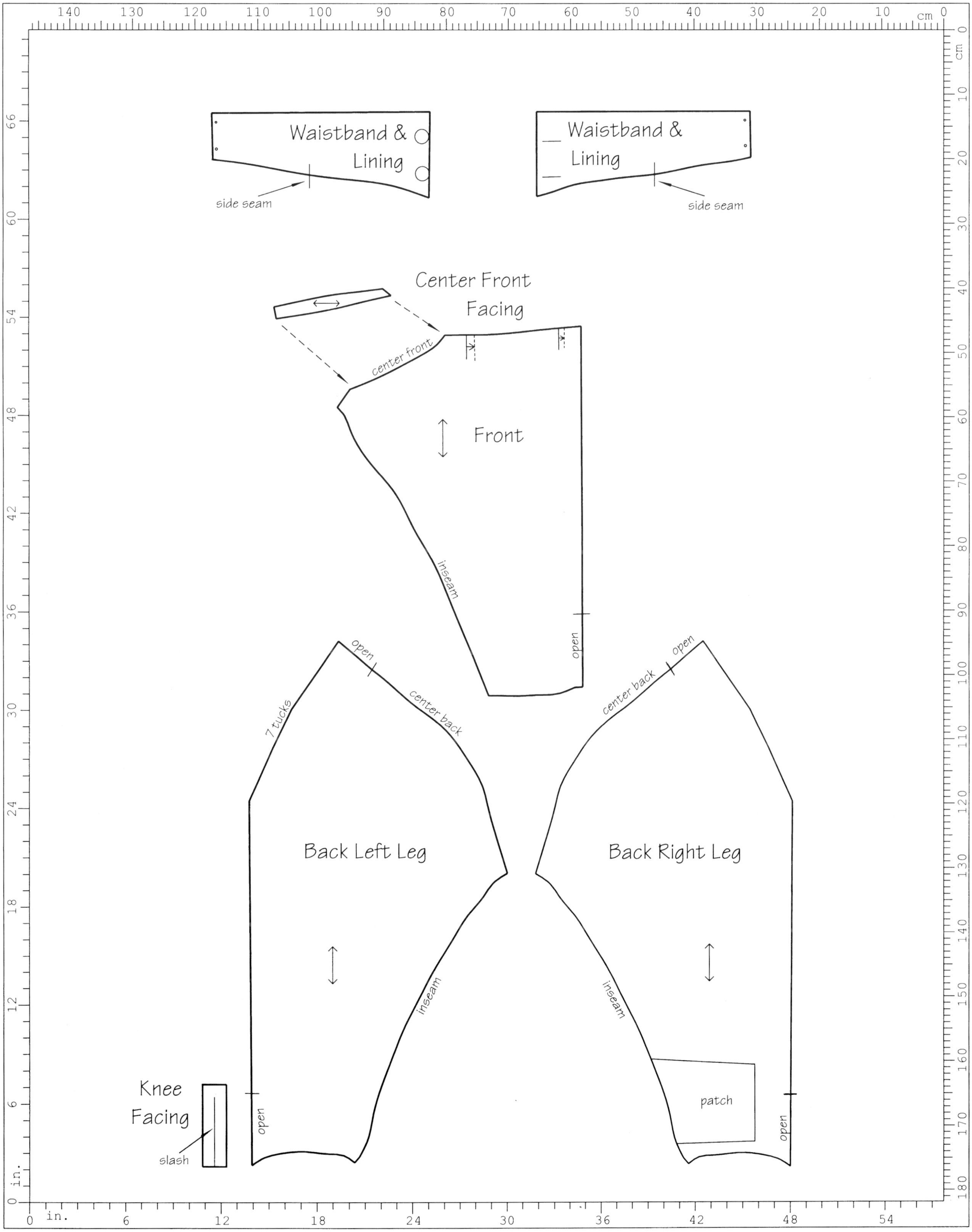
Waistband &
Lining
side seam
Waistband &
Lining
side seam
Center Front
Facing
center front
Front
inseam
open
open
7 tucks
center back
Back Left Leg
inseam
open
open
center back
Back Right Leg
inseam
patch
open
Knee
Facing
slash
cm
in.

❦ 24
STOCK

England, 1740–1760

White linen; red silk marking thread; linen sewing thread

Overall length, 17" (43.2 cm); width, 2" (5 cm)

Accession number: 1993-166

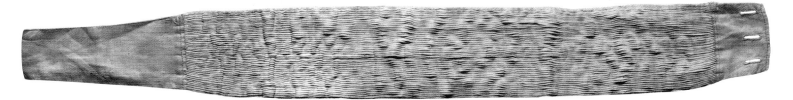

White linen stock trimmed with forty-five minute pleats.

An ancestor of the modern necktie, the stock fastened around the neck over the shirtband or collar. The tabs at either end were intended for a metal stock buckle whose knobs were buttoned through the buttonholes on the stock. The tapered tab extension was drawn through the buckle and cinched to the correct length.

This stock came with an envelope attesting that it had belonged to George II, king of England from 1727 to 1760. Although the envelope dates to the nineteenth century and therefore is inconclusive as documentation, the cross-stitched crown and fine workmanship and materials suggest that the history may be true. The letter itself is missing.

Materials

The stock is made from white linens of exceptional quality. The tab thread count is approximately 100 by 140 threads per inch (2.5 cm). Linen of even finer texture is pleated to the front. The sewing thread is linen, and the marking thread is brownish red silk.

Change over Time

The stock is in remarkably good condition, though slightly distorted. It is missing the stiffening material that kept it from collapsing under the chin while worn.

Detail of tabs to be fastened at the back of the neck. The mark is a crown surmounting the number 46. The stock has a history of ownership by George II, king of England.

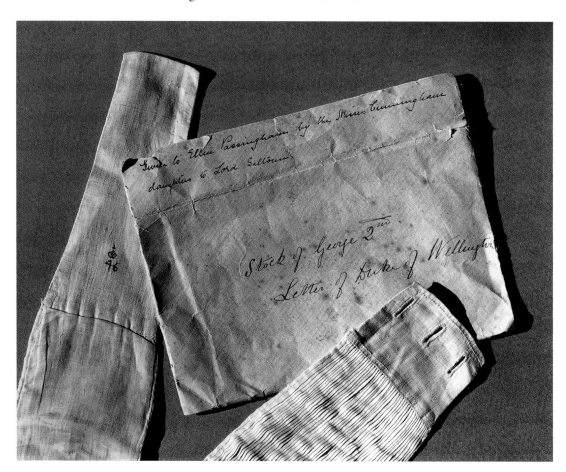

1993-166

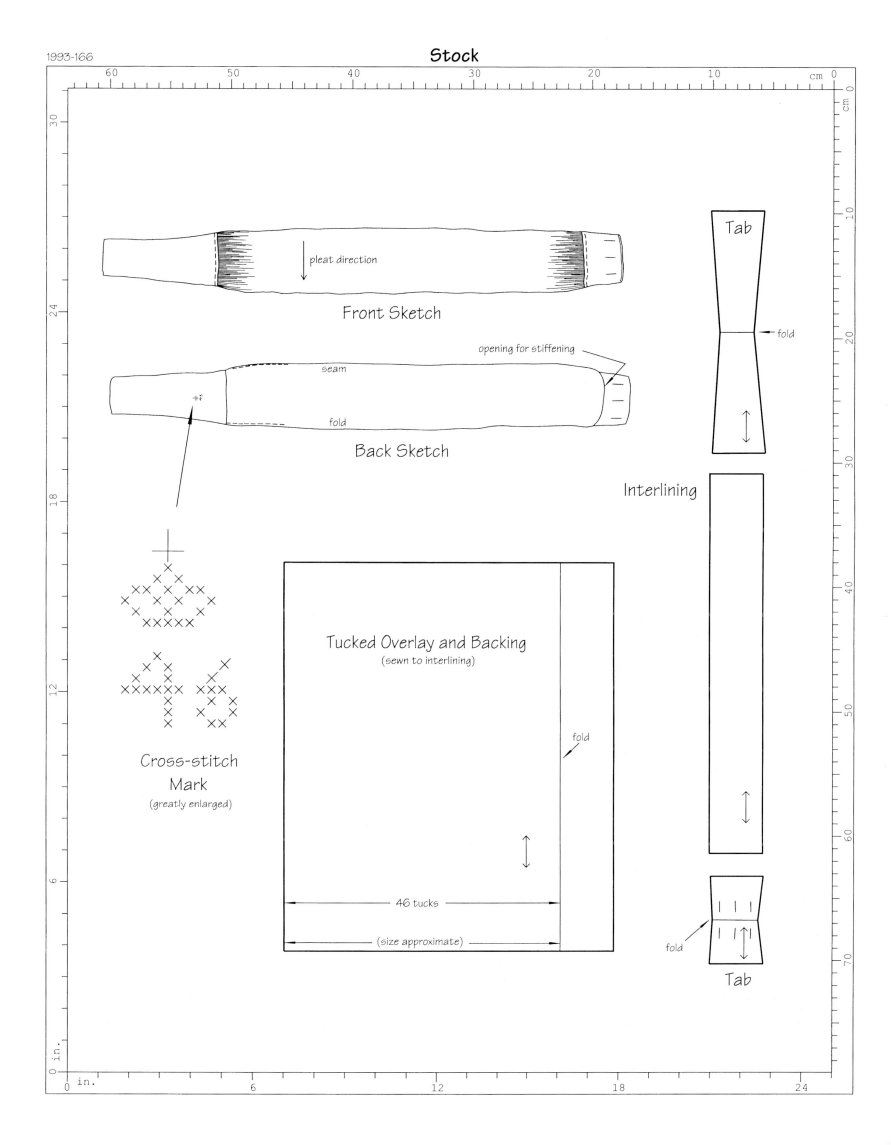

pleat direction

Front Sketch

opening for stiffening

seam

fold

Back Sketch

Tab

fold

Interlining

Tucked Overlay and Backing
(sewn to interling)

fold

Cross-stitch
Mark
(greatly enlarged)

46 tucks

(size approximate)

fold

Tab

Construction

Right: *Silver stock buckle worn in Virginia ca. 1790. The three round knobs slip through buttonholes on the stock tab. One of the prongs is missing.*

Stitching: The stock is stitched with running stitches, whipstitches, backstitches, buttonhole stitches, and cross-stitches.

Tucked Layer: The stock consists of three layers fastened to tapering tabs at either end. A rectangle of very fine, semisheer linen is pleated into forty-six tucks and sewn to a coarser linen interlining with long running stitches. Each pleat measures about $\frac{1}{32}$" (1 mm) in width and takes up about $\frac{5}{32}$" (4 mm) of fabric.

Backing: The third layer is an extension of the tucked layer. The extension is folded over the interlining and brought around to the back. It is left open at one end to receive stiffening.

Tabs: Each tab is a double layer of linen, folded at the ends, with the raw edges of the sides turned in and stitched. This stitching was done with minute whipstitches, worked from the top after the raw edges were pressed in toward each other. The pieces were not sewn with right sides together and turned. Very fine backstitches are worked a scant $\frac{1}{8}$" (2 to 3 mm) from the edge, where the tabs join the stock proper. One tab has three buttonholes for the knobs of a stock buckle; the buttonholes are worked with linen buttonhole stitches. The button-hole tab is topstitched across the end. The longer tab has very fine cross-stitching in brownish red that forms a crown and the number 46.

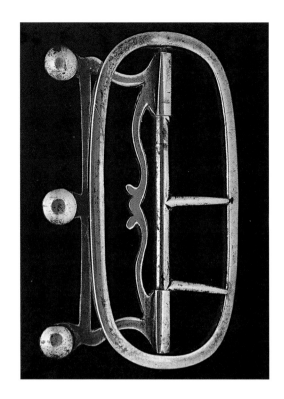

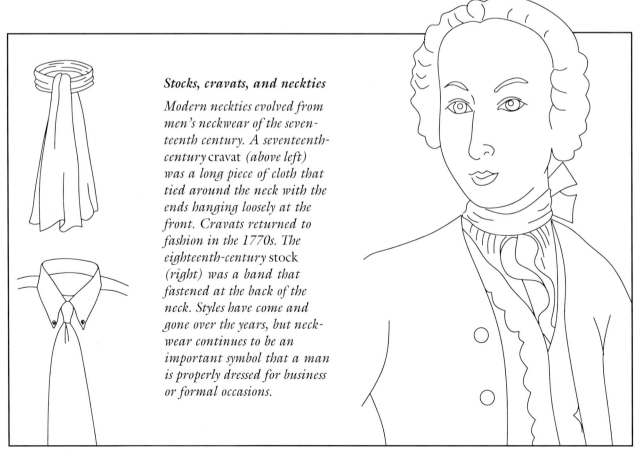

Stocks, cravats, and neckties

Modern neckties evolved from men's neckwear of the seventeenth century. A seventeenth-century cravat *(above left) was a long piece of cloth that tied around the neck with the ends hanging loosely at the front. Cravats returned to fashion in the 1770s. The eighteenth-century* stock *(right) was a band that fastened at the back of the neck. Styles have come and gone over the years, but neckwear continues to be an important symbol that a man is properly dressed for business or formal occasions.*

25

CAP

Europe, 1740–1760

Brown ribbed silk embroidered with silk; linen; paper; striped silk and worsted lining; silk cord trim; silk and linen sewing threads

Overall height, approximately 6" (15.2 cm); circumference, 23½" (59.7 cm)

Accession number: G1991-499, Gift of Cora Ginsburg

Caps were worn indoors and out by men of all social levels. They were informal replacements for the wig and cocked hat. Working men wore simple caps of linen or wool when a felt hat with a brim was too hot or cumbersome. Men of leisure wore more elegant caps indoors to cover their shaved heads when they weren't wearing their wigs. Close-fitting caps were worn to bed to keep the head warm in cold rooms heated only by fireplaces.

This cap has a fascinating inside story, for it is interlined with old recycled paper cut from an eighteenth-century book written in Latin. The work is a reprint of a picturesque but inaccurate biography of Alexander the Great by the first-century author Quintus Curtius Rufus. The biography was printed in various editions in English and Latin. (Recycled old manuscripts have been found inside other artifacts as well, including furniture and keyboard instruments. In the nineteenth century, old paper was used for quilt templates.)

Man's brown silk cap embroidered with multicolored silks.

Materials

This fitted cap with shaped cuffs is made of brown, heavy ribbed silk embroidered with multicolor silk flowers. The cuffs are stiffened with interlinings of heavy rag paper resembling light cardboard and lined with sized brown linen. The slightly peaked crown is stiffened with recycled book paper. The crown is lined with a plain-woven, silk-and-worsted striped fabric. Silk cording covers the seams. Flowerlike tassels of metallic silver wound around strips of vellum form an ornament at the peak. The cap is sewn with brown silk, gold silk, and natural-color linen.

Change over Time

The embroidered silk pieces are slightly puckered, and the cap is distorted. The striped lining material is torn around the edges where it meets the cuff, revealing the paper interlining. The paper has become curled and ragged over the years.

Construction

Stitching: All of the seams are sewn with running stitches. Silk cording is couched from the outside

over the crown seams and the undulating edge of the cuffs using gold-color silk thread.

Embroidery: The embroidery was worked with fine silk floss using satin, shaded satin, feather, and straight stitches. The colors include pink shaded to cream, greens, reds, blues, and black. The colors and details vary slightly from panel to panel. The embroidery was done to the desired shapes, then the pieces were cut and sewn together with brown silk thread.

Cuffs: The two shaped and embroidered cuffs were basted to heavy rag-paper stiffening. Cuff linings of glazed and sized linen were placed over the stiffening, turned under, and slip-stitched from the outside at the undulating top edges. The lower edges of the cuff linings were basted in place without being turned under, ending short of the cuff bottom. These unfinished edges were hidden when the assembled cuff was attached to the cap with long running stitches, catching the cuff lining to

Detail of 1775 French print showing a storekeeper in a cap.

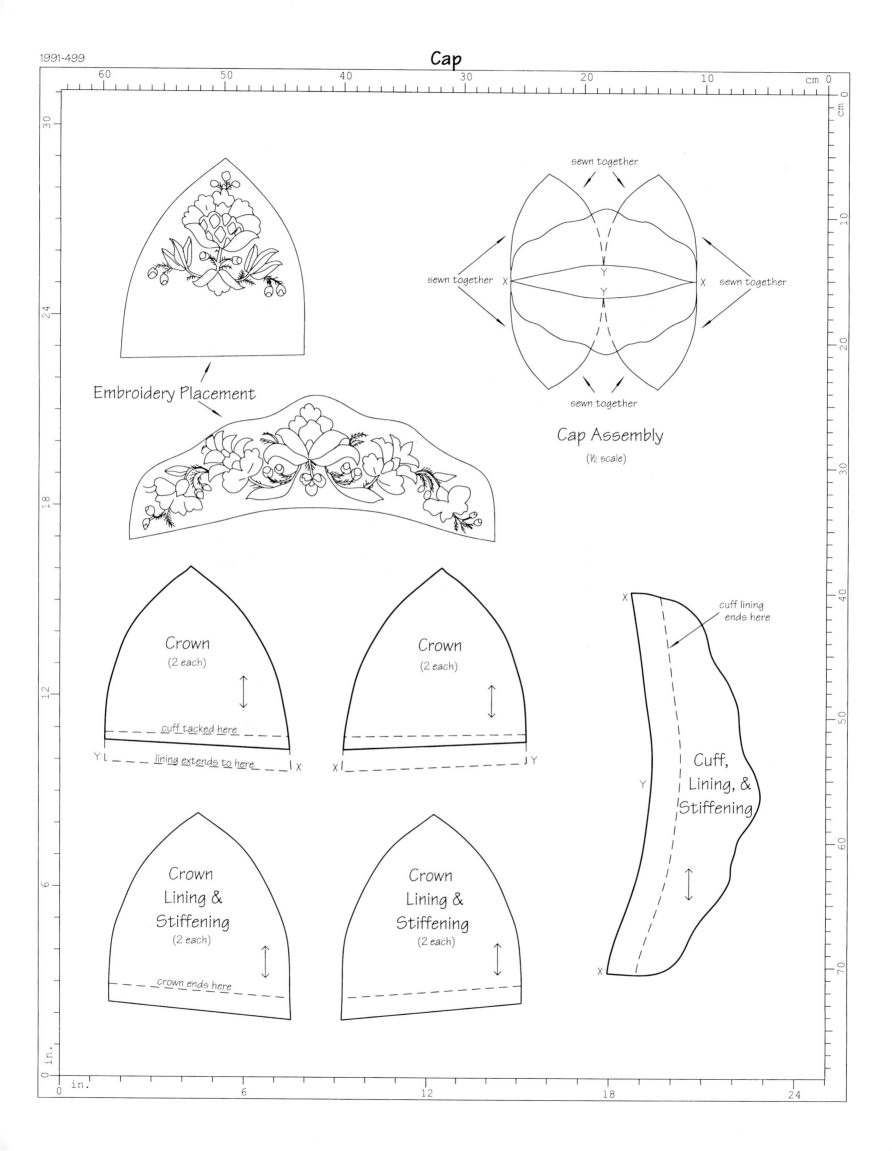

Embroidery Placement

sewn together

sewn together X — Y — X sewn together

sewn together

Cap Assembly

(½ scale)

Crown
(2 each)

Crown
(2 each)

cuff tacked here

Y — lining extends to here — X

X — Y

cuff lining
ends here

Crown
Lining &
Stiffening
(2 each)

Crown
Lining &
Stiffening
(2 each)

crown ends here

X

Cuff,
Lining, &
Stiffening

Y

X

the embroidered silk. It is typical of the period that fabric was not wasted where it could not be seen. In this cap, both the cuff linings and the embroidered crown pieces stop short of the cap bottom, where they would not be visible.

Crown: The brown embroidered crown pieces are sewn with silk, and the crown lining is sewn with natural-color linen. The striped crown lining is basted to book-paper stiffening. The paper interlin-ings and striped linings extended longer than the embroidered exterior pieces. During final assembly, they were turned under and slip-stitched to the fin-ished cuffs. The cap is topped with two metallic, looped tassels made of silver thread wound around a vellum base.

Assembly: When assembled, the long sides of the crown pieces and the cuff ends meet at X. The short sides meet at the center of the cuff, Y. 🦟

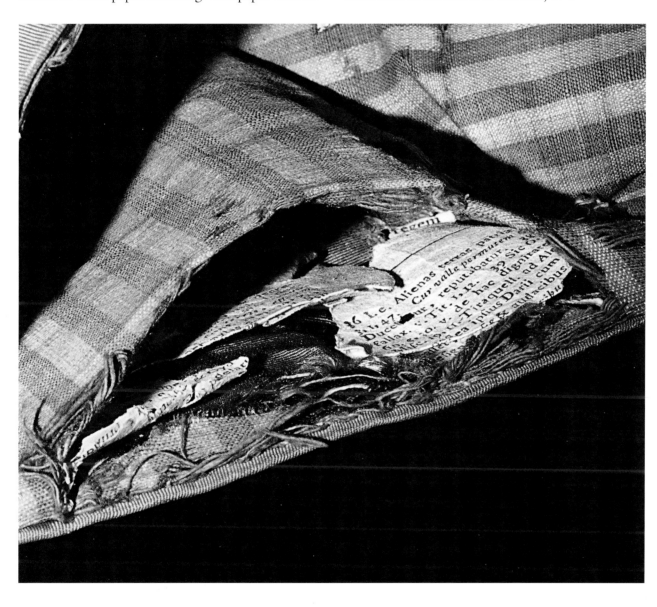

Striped cap lining and printed paper interlin-ing visible through a tear in the lining.

117

Cap Embroidery Pattern

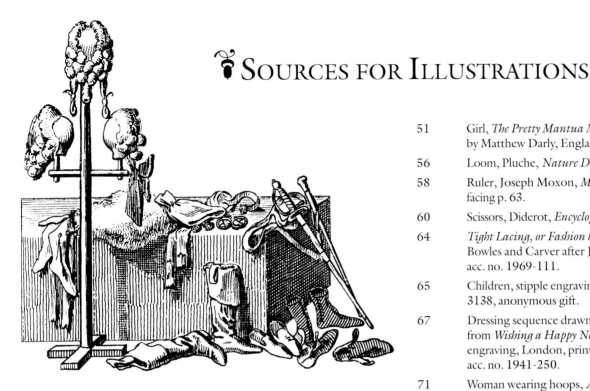

❦ Sources for Illustrations

Except as noted, all illustrations are from materials in the collections of the Colonial Williamsburg Foundation, including the Department of Collections, Special Collections at the John D. Rockefeller, Jr. Library, and the Abby Aldrich Rockefeller Folk Art Center. Some of the images were adapted from the authors' photographs.

Page

5 Line drawings of couples adapted from *Astronomy*, line engraving, printed for F. Bull, London, ca. 1750, acc. no. 1959-430,2; *Graham's Lady's and Gentleman's Magazine*, February, 1842; and Hal L. Cohen, ed., *1922 Montgomery Ward Catalogue . . .* ([New York], 1969), pp. 35, 253.

14 Pinking iron, acc. no. G1971-2049, anonymous gift.

19 Brocading on loom, Denis Diderot, *Encyclopédie . . . Recueil de Planches . . .*, 11 vols. plus supplement (Paris, 1762–1777), XI, "Soierie," plate LXIV. Hereafter cited as Diderot, *Encyclopédie . . . Planches*.

20 Sack back drawn from gown, acc. no. 1953-848.

33 Glazing press, Noël Antoine Pluche, *Spectacle de la Nature: or, Nature Display'd . . .*, VI (London, 1748), plate XVI. Hereafter cited as Pluche, *Nature Display'd*.

37 Petticoat, acc. no. G1986-55, gift of Cora Ginsburg.

38 *The Gypsie Fortune-Teller*, black-and-white mezzotint, printed for R. Sayer and J. Bennett, London, 1783, acc. no. 1960-201.

Block-printed cotton-and-linen textile, acc. no. G1974-370, bequest of Mrs. Jason Westerfield.

42 Woman, *La Pharmacie Rustique*, line and stipple engraving on paper, Barthelemi Hubner, France, 1775, acc. no. 1959-437.

Girl in profile, Diderot, *Encyclopédie . . . Planches*, supplement, s.v. "Couturière."

43 Woman, *Modern Love II: The Elopement*, J. Goldar and T. Bradford after John Collet, England, 1765, acc. no. 1969-100.

47 Apron, acc. no. G1971-1539, anonymous gift.

51 Cloak patterns, Diderot, *Encyclopédie . . . Planches,* supplement, s.v. "Marchande de Modes."

51 Girl, *The Pretty Mantua Maker*, hand-colored etching, published by Matthew Darly, England, 1772, acc. no. 1955-62, 32.

56 Loom, Pluche, *Nature Display'd*, plate XI.

58 Ruler, Joseph Moxon, *Mechanick Exercises* (London, 1703), facing p. 63.

60 Scissors, Diderot, *Encyclopédie . . . Planches*, IV, "Gantier," plate V.

64 *Tight Lacing, or Fashion before Ease*, hand-colored mezzotint, Bowles and Carver after John Collet, England, 1770–1775, acc. no. 1969-111.

65 Children, stipple engraving, London, ca. 1790, acc. no. G1971-3138, anonymous gift.

67 Dressing sequence drawn by authors. The dressed girl is adapted from *Wishing a Happy New Year to Grand Papa*, mezzotint engraving, London, printed for John Bowles, ca. 1750, acc. no. 1941-250.

71 Woman wearing hoops, *Architecture*, hand-colored line engraving, J. Boydel, London, ca. 1750, acc. no. 1959-430, 1.

74 Mitts, acc. nos. 1985-214, 1985-210, 1985-241, 1985-213, G1971-3182, anonymous gift.

75 Leg, Diderot, *Encyclopédie . . . Planches*, supplement, "Cordonnier," plate II.

78 Stocking clocks graphed by Carol E. Harrison.

79 Stocking frame, Diderot, *Encyclopédie . . . Planches*, II, "Faiseur de Métier à Bas," plate I.

Woman, detail, William Hogarth, *A Rake's Progress*, plate II, line engraving on paper, London, 1735, acc. no. 1951-91.

81 Tailor, detail, line engraving by Daniel Chodowiecki in Jean Bernard Basedow, *Elementarwerke fur Die Jugend und ihre Freunde* (Berlin and Dessau, 1774), plate XIX. Hereafter cited as Chodowiecki.

87 Horseman, Diderot, *Encyclopédie . . . Planches*, VII, "Manège et Equitation," plate IV.

89 Buttons, Diderot, *Encyclopédie . . . Planches,* IX, "Tailleur d'Habits," plate VII.

97 Man, *Magasin des Modes Nouvelles, Française et Anglaises* (June 30, 1787), acc. no. G1971-2298, anonymous gift.

98 Embroiderers, Diderot, *Encyclopédie . . . Planches*, II, "Brodeur," plate I.

104 Man, detail, Chodowiecki, plate XXVI.

105 Man, detail, Diderot, *Encyclopédie . . . Planches*, V, "Fonderie des Canons," plate XV.

108 Shirt drawing taken from an early nineteenth-century shirt, acc. no. G1989-401, gift of Cora Ginsburg.

110 Man in underwear, adapted from Chodowiecki, plate LIV.

114 Man wearing stock drawn from William Dering, *George Booth as a Young Man*, oil on canvas, Virginia, 1740–1750, acc. no. 1975-242.

115 Man in profile, detail, *La Pharmacie Rustique;* see note for p. 42.

119–120 Clothes, Chodowiecki, plate III, adapted by the authors.

🐞 END NOTES

Page

8   *Le point à rabattre sous la main* is illustrated in Denis Diderot, *Encyclopédie . . . Recueil de Planches . . .* , 11 vols. plus supplement (Paris, 1762–1777), IX, "Tailleur d'Habits," plate IX. Hereafter cited as Diderot, *Encyclopédie . . . Planches.* The authors thank Richard Hill for pointing out the relationship of this plate to the stitch used on men's tailored garments. Mr. Hill translates the stitch name as the "underhand hem stitch."

11   John Singleton Copley, *Mary and Elizabeth Royall*, oil on canvas, Wadsworth Athenaeum, Hartford, Conn.

33   Ursula Priestley, "The Norwich Textile Industry, 1750–1880," in Pamela Clabburn, *The Norwich Shawl* (London: Norfolk Museum Service, 1995), p. 2.

38   "Charleston oyster seller named Phillis . . ." *South-Carolina and American General Gazette* (Charleston), January 12–19, 1776.

42   "Callico Jacket without Cuffs . . ." *Maryland Gazette* (Annapolis), September 6, 1770.

43   "A convict servant . . ." Rind's *Virginia Gazette* (Williamsburg), July 20, 1769.

     "The young slave maid . . ." Julian P. Boyd et al., eds., *The Papers of Thomas Jefferson*, XI (Princeton, N. J., 1955), p. 574.

56   Broadcloth was required to be 63" wide according to a British law passed during the reign of Edward VI.

61   The authors thank Nancy Glass for sharing information about lacing stays.

65   "On a hot July day . . ." Hunter Dickinson Farish, ed., *Journal & Letters of Philip Vickers Fithian . . .* (Williamsburg, Va., 1957), p. 150.

69   The authors thank Kathleen Eagen Johnson of Historic Hudson Valley for genealogical information on the Van Rensselaer family.

74   "A milliner in Williamsburg . . ." Rind's *Va. Gaz.*, October 6, 1768.

75   "2 Dozn. of White Ribed Silk Hose . . ." Frances Norton Mason, ed., *John Norton & Sons . . .* (Richmond, Va., 1937), p. 218.

79   "By 1750 there were an estimated fourteen thousand stocking frames . . ." S. D. Chapman, "The Genesis of the British Hosiery Industry, 1650–1750," *Textile History*, III (1972), p. 7.

     "Those [stockings] that have been made . . ." Purdie and Dixon's *Va. Gaz.*, June 3, 1773.

     "Robert Carter of Nomini Hall set up . . ." Patricia A. Gibbs, "Cloth Production in Virginia to 1800" (research report, Colonial Williamsburg Foundation, 1978), pp. 33–36.

81   "Jonathan Prosser advertised . . ." Rind's *Va. Gaz.*, July 21, 1768.

     "The cloths you sent . . ." Robert Carter, Williamsburg, Va., to Robert Cornthwaite, London, March 25, 1765. Quoted in Susan Briggs Ely, "Robert Carter Letterbook, 1764–1768" (M. A. thesis, College of William and Mary, 1962), p. 9.

102 "Virginian Robert 'King' Carter . . ." Quoted by Victor Dennis Golladay, "The Nicholas Family in Virginia" (Ph.D. diss., University of Virginia, 1973), p. 53.

109 "Thomas Jefferson's drawers . . ." The drawers are illustrated in Linda Baumgarten, "Under Waistcoats and Drawers," *Dress*, XIX (1992), p. 13.

110 Men's underwear . . . , discussed ibid.